Black Bass

JOHN ALDEN KNIGHT

Black Bass

Skyhorse Publishing

Skyhorse Publishing books may be purchased in bulk at special discounts
for sales promotion, corporate gifts, fund-raising, or educational
purposes. Special editions can also be created to specifications. For
details, contact the Special Sales Department, Skyhorse Publishing, 307
West 36th Street, 11th Floor, New York, NY 10018 or
info@skyhorsepublishing.com.

Skyhorse® and Skyhorse Publishing® are registered trademarks of
Skyhorse Publishing, Inc.®, a Delaware corporation.

www.skyhorsepublishing.com

10 9 8 7 6 5 4 3 2 1

Library of Congress Cataloging-in-Publication Data is available on file.

ISBN: 978-1-62914-167-1

Ebook ISBN: 978-1-62914-308-8

Cover design by: Richard Rossiter

Printed in the United States of America

To my Friend
Edgar Burke

Acknowledgments

~~~~~~

BOTH THE PUBLISHER and the author are indebted to many people for material that appears in this book: to Dr. Edgar Burke for the beautiful color plates; to Harold Bush for the line drawings and sketches; to O. Jay Blake, Earnest Hille, and others for the photography; to *Field & Stream, Sports Afield, Outdoor Life,* and *Outdoors* for permission to rewrite and use some of the material that appears herein; to Jason Lucas, whose writings have been quoted here and there; to Dr. Carl L. Hubbs and Dr. Reeve M. Bailey for their aid in the discussion of classification; and to Dr. Francesca LaMonte who put up with all too many questions that were over my depth in matters of ichthyology.

Last but by no means least, the author wishes to express his gratitude to a multitude of fellow anglers from whom a great many items of bass lore have been gleaned during half a century of diligent angling.

Contents

Illustrations

~~~~~~

xi

Introduction

▲▲▲

To ATTEMPT TO put together a book that deals with bass in
general and to enumerate, describe, and set down the individual characteristics of each and every member of the bass
family, great and small, would indeed be a stupendous task.
Further, to itemize and explain the unending permutations
of angling methods incidental to the capture of all of the
members of the bass family not only would test the knowledge and ability of the writer, but would, I'm afraid, be a
sore trial to the reader. Between the Spotted Jewfish or
Giant Sea Bass on one hand and the lowly Pumpkinseed on
the other, the bass family runs the full gamut of size, color,
weight, and distribution. Even with the dozens of varieties
that are scientifically established today, the list is still far from
being complete.

With this multiplicity of subspecies in mind, the title of
this book—*Black Bass*—was chosen carefully. By dealing only
with the black basses, we thereby narrowed the list down
considerably. But don't be deceived. Contrary to general
opinion, the black basses do not confine themselves to two
main varieties, the Largemouth and the Smallmouth. So that
we can understand each other more thoroughly, here is the
accepted list of the black basses—the *Micropterini*.

Black Bass

Family Centrarchidae Cope
  Subfamily 1. Lepominae Gill
    Tribe 1. Micropterini (new name)
      Genus 1. *Micropterus* Lacépède
        1. *M. punctulatus* (Rafinesque), spotted bass
          1a. *M.p. punctulatus* (Rafinesque), northern spotted bass
          1b. *M.p. henshalli,* new subspecies, Alabama spotted bass
          1c. *M.p. wichitae,* new subspecies, Wichita spotted bass
        2. *M. coosae,* new species, redeyed bass
        3. *M. dolomieu* Lacépède, smallmouthed bass
          3a. *M. d. velox,* new subspecies, Neosho smallmouthed bass
          3b. *M. d. dolomieu* Lacépède, northern smallmouthed bass
      Genus 2. *Huro* Cuvier
        4. *H. salmoides* (Lacépède), largemouthed bass (Subspecies not yet delimited)

Please note the last line of this enumeration, the one in parentheses. Since the listing was made in 1940, another subspecies has been added, the Texas Spotted Bass, *Micropterus punctulatus treculii* (Vaillant and Bocourt).

While we are about it, let's set something straight which has needed straightening for a long, long time. A little learning is a very dangerous thing. Too many men, when they take pen in hand, indulge themselves in what might be called "lay classification" of our game fishes. In other words, they attempt to classify by using common names. Classification simply cannot be done by this method.

How many times have you seen this statement in print? "The Brook Trout is not a 'trout' at all. He is a 'char.'" Well, Brook Trout, Brown Trout, Rainbow Trout, what have you, all belong to the *Salmo* family.

Introduction

This sort of thing happens all too often. It has been said, "A Black Bass isn't a Bass at all. He's a Sunfish," and, "A Black Bass isn't a Bass. In reality, he's a Perch." All of which is completely and beautifully haywire. If you want to use common names, a Black Bass is a Black Bass; a Sunfish is a Sunfish, and a Perch is a Perch. All of these fish belong to the suborder *Percoidei*. The Largemouth, the Smallmouth, and the Pumpkinseed all come under the general classification Centrarchidae, which is referred to as the Sunfish family. But that doesn't mean that a Black Bass is a Sunfish or a Perch any more than the fact that I belong to the order *Homo sapiens* means that I am an African or a Chinaman. As I say, there are a great many game fish, in both fresh and salt water, which properly can be listed as Bass, and for our purposes it is safer to stick to common names and not confuse matters.

This being in no sense a scientific work, it will not be necessary to include scientific descriptions of the various members of the list. For the most part, we are concerned only with two of its members—the Largemouthed and the Smallmouthed Bass. If you want all the data on the Bass family, complete with biological keys, go to your library and ask for *A Revision of the Black Basses* (Micropterus *and* Huro) *with Descriptions of Four New Forms* by Carl L. Hubbs and Reeve M. Bailey, published by the University of Michigan Press, Ann Arbor, Michigan, July 27, 1940. Subsequently these two gentlemen published through the same press Brochure Number 457, *Subspecies of Spotted Bass* (Micropterus punctulatus) *in Texas*, February 10, 1942. These two able works will give you all that you need to know, or *can* know, for that matter, of the scientific aspects of the Back Basses.

Incidentally, I'm not at all sure that there isn't some work that can be done on Smallmouth subspecies. While the following account is by no means conclusive, it may very well be that there is an interesting breed of Smallmouth which is known at present to only a few people.

Black Bass

Throughout the lower valley of the main Delaware River, and particularly in the vicinity of the little village of Mast Hope, Pennsylvania, the old-timers will tell you some tall tales of the "Oregon Bass," which, according to local belief, show up in the Delaware every seven years. These fish are reputed to grow to prodigious sizes, specimens ranging from twelve to fifteen pounds not being uncommon. They are not the same color as the regular Delaware Smallmouth. Instead, they are said to take on a greenish yellow tinge, with no appreciable darking across the back of the fish. Other than that, they look and act like ordinary oversize Smallmouth.

I have never seen one of these fish, but I have heard about them from two different sources. My first informant was a man who was employed in the railroad shops at Susquehanna, Pennsylvania. We fell to talking about bass and bass fishing while we were each having a cup of miserable coffee at a lunch counter in Susquehanna. We had agreed that it was a sad but inescapable fact that most lunch counters served horrible coffee, when he noticed the fishing license button in my hat. He then told me that he planned to go fishing that week end, down in Mast Hope eddy in the main Delaware. I asked him why he went so far to fish for bass when the North Branch of the Susquehanna River flowed right through town. Then he told me of the Oregon Bass, that year, according to him, being the magic seventh year when these fish were in the river. The weights he mentioned so casually—nine, ten, twelve pounds—were so much at variance with anything I had learned of Smallmouth sizes that I charged it up to optimism of a fishing fanatic and promptly forgot it.

The next time I heard of Oregon Bass was, of all places, in the clubrooms of the Anglers' Club of New York. As a rule, you don't hear much about bass at the Anglers' Club. There the discussion runs to salmon or trout. Bass are "coarse fish" and of little interest to the general run of the members. Were it not for the fact that the story was told to me by

Introduction

a reliable individual, I would hesitate to set it down here. However, he is a friend of many years' standing, the very soul of honesty, and his word is good with me up to any amount of my somewhat limited financial resources. Unfortunately, the story was told to him by the man who saw the fish and had it weighed. Offsetting this third-hand version is the fact that my friend vouches for the reliability of the teller, just as I vouch for my friend. I have every reason to believe that it is true, otherwise I would have forgotten it long since.

This man, who is an executive in one of New York's publishing houses, had taken a camp at Mast Hope for the summer. It being too much of a journey for him to attempt daily commutation, he stayed throughout the week at his house in Orange, New Jersey, and over each week end joined his wife and his two sons at the camp at Mast Hope, arriving there on Friday afternoon.

It so happened that there was divided opinion in that household concerning the merits of the sport of angling. The father and one of the sons could see no virtue in fishing, while the mother and the other youngster, a boy of twelve, were quite fond of it. These two knew little or nothing about fishing, but they liked it and each day found them on the river. Their tackle consisted of a heavy hand line and a big pickerel spoon. With this rig they trolled up and down Mast Hope eddy and they managed to bring in enough bass and walleye to supply their table.

One Friday these two were trolling, the mother rowing and the boy holding the line, when they had a heavy strike. The mother soon saw that the fish was too big for the youngster to handle. He was game all right but not strong enough for the task. Before they could change places, the heavy line had cut the boy's hands several times. After a nip-and-tuck battle that lasted for a considerable time, she was able to pull the big fish into the shallows. There the boy threw himself

xvii

on it and between the two of them they managed to get it up on dry land.

Having no live box and no ice for refrigeration at camp, they had been keeping their fish in a large burlap sack that was tied securely with heavy rope and allowed to rest on the river bottom, out where the current could bring a constant supply of fresh water. Into this bag went the big bass, to be saved until the man of the house could see it.

He showed up, as usual, on the afternoon train, and was escorted immediately to the riverbank. Together the three of them carried the fish, still in the bag, to the local store where, still alive, it was placed on the scales. The reading showed that the big bass weighed well over fourteen pounds. It was then that the storekeeper and several interested spectators agreed that it was one of the Oregon Bass. All professed to know the species well and were not too greatly impressed by its size.

After that the man took the fish to camp. There he cut off the head and tail, dressed it out, scaled it, and cut it into three big chunks. One of them was baked for dinner that night. The other two pieces were placed in the store refrigerator.

Sunday afternoon, the family broke camp and came home. They had another meal of baked bass from the second chunk, and the third was given to a neighbor where it provided a meal for a family of four.

The man, knowing that my friend was interested in fishing, told him the story while they were riding to New York on the train one morning during the following week, and my friend, knowing my interest in bass, told me.

Of course, my friend took the man to task for destroying such an unusual fish. He was truly disturbed when he learned that he had unknowingly deprived his son of what very probably would have been a world's record Smallmouth. However, the damage had been done. All I can do now is to

Introduction

give you the details here as they were told to me. It is barely possible—not probable, but possible—that some interesting things might develop if some scientific work were done in the lower Delaware.

As stated earlier, this is not a scientific work. Let us, then, leave the scientific aspects of Black Bass to the scientists, where they belong, and go on to see what we can find out about the habits, behavior, and characteristics of Largemouth and Smallmouth Bass, and of angling methods incidental to their capture.

Black Bass

CHAPTER I

The Yearly Cycle

THE LARGEMOUTH BASS is classified as a warm-water fish. Unlike most fresh-water game fish, a Largemouth is perfectly happy in temperatures that range well up into the nineties. He's a lazy sort of a fellow and he doesn't seem to care for running water. Instead, he prefers ponds, lakes, and slow-flowing rivers. A mud bottom is entirely to his liking and he is equally content in shallow or deep water just so long as that water is still, or comparatively so. It is not uncommon to find both Largemouth and Smallmouth in the same lake or pond but it *is* unusual in such a pond to find Largemouth living in water that is typically Smallmouth water or Small-mouth living in the mud-bottom shallows that the Large-mouth prefer.

An excellent example of this typical choice of water can be seen in Mystery Pond near Newport, Vermont. Technically, that is not its correct name, but the only other name I have heard for it is "the power dam" and so we christened it Mystery Pond. This body of water, as you may have surmised, is an artificial lake that was created when the City of Newport dammed the Clyde River to supply power for the generation of electricity. I suppose that the lake covers about twenty-five or thirty acres in all—maybe more if you want to include the rather extensive swamp at one end. Before the area was flooded, a goodly portion of it first had to be lumbered. This was done pretty much without thought to the fishing that was to take place there in later years. The big trees were cut down, the usable timber was trucked out, and the stumps, useless logs, and piles of slashing were left there, just as they fell. Then the area was flooded. It is with mingled and conflicting emotions of pleasure and regret that I recall how many heavy bass and how much good and costly terminal tackle have departed from me and from my son, Dick, in the tangled mazes of those cursed piles of waterlogged slashing. To be sure, we continue to fish there because that is where the bass are, but the fact remains that those piles of slashing are indeed a collective trial and tribulation that will try the very souls of far more patient men than I.

As I say, Mystery Pond was and is a splendid example of the mutually satisfactory way that Largemouth and Smallmouth Bass divvy up a bass pond. At the mouth of the inlet where there are log tangles, mossy rocks, and a flow of fresh, cool water, the Smallmouth take up residence. On down through the deep ravine of the old river channel they live and we catch them along that deep-water bank clear down to the point. Here the old channel curves and makes its way across the bottom of the lake proper toward the breast of the dam. In all the hundreds of times I have fished it, neither I nor any of my companions has caught a Smallmouth downstream from the point where the channel curves out across the pond.

In the backwaters, coves, and out across the shallow stump-covered flats the Largemouth live. To be sure, we catch Largemouth along the deep-water bank between the point and the river mouth, but the closer we come to the inlet, with its smooth flow of cool running water, the fewer Largemouth we find. And not once have we taken one from the inlet mouth proper. It is almost as though territorial boundaries have been

The Yearly Cycle

established and lines drawn over which neither species dares to venture into the domain of the other.

The habits of the northern Largemouth differ from those of the southern Largemouth in that the former hibernates during the winter months. When the "ice goes out" from the lakes and streams of the northern latitudes, the Largemouth Bass are buried snugly in the muddy bottoms of the backwaters and deep coves, away from possible effects of floods that would interrupt their long winter sleep. Not until the water temperatures are up in the neighborhood of fifty or fifty-five degrees do they wake up and come out of hibernation.

Not always is it possible for bass to find convenient backwaters that have deep, muddy bottoms. Then the bass must use what makeshifts they can contrive. Holes in stumps or in waterlogged logs, nooks and crannies between the rocks, crevasses between ledges, in fact, any sort of a protective opening will serve to shelter a hibernating bass in case he can not find the ideal wintering ground.

Hibernation is not always confined to the winter months. When an emergency arises, bass resort to hibernation as a means of self-preservation. It is nothing short of amazing how much adversity a bass can undergo and still emerge right side up and apparently none the worse for the experience.

The summer of 1937 was a particularly dry and hot one, especially in southern New York State and north-central Pennsylvania. Trout streams dried up completely and bass rivers fell far below the danger point. The loss of fish during these two unfortunate months was incalculable. The West Branch of the Delaware, being in reality an oversize trout stream, dried up until it was a mere trickle. Not only that, but the warm weather brought on an unprecedented crop of algae. In the hot, low water, this vegetable matter decomposed and fermented until what water there was took on the

5

Black Bass

aspect of thick pea soup and smelled to high heaven. True to form, the bass took to the mud and there they stayed until welcome rains brought the water back to normal. Having seen the river some three weeks earlier when my favorite pools could be crossed dry-shod, I assembled my tackle with misgivings. To my great and delighted surprise, I found the bass to be present in their usual numbers and the fishing unaffected.

In one of the early reports of the Fisheries, Game and Forest Commission of the State of New York appears an account of the remarkable capacity for survival that a black bass possesses. At one of the hatcheries, a holding pool that had been used to store adult black bass was drained one fall and allowed to stand dry and empty throughout the winter months. Of course, before this was done the bass were seined out—or so the hatchery men thought. The following spring the pool was flooded again and in it were placed several thousand small trout.

One June evening the hatchery men were surprised to see some large fish slashing about among the trout, evidently feeding on the small fish.

The next day, allowing the water to remain at the same level, they seined the pool with a net that had a mesh large enough to allow the trout to pass through. Much to their surprise, they captured four bass that weighed from two to three pounds each. There being no other way for the fish to get into the pool, it being adequately screened and fed from a two-inch pipe, the only way for those bass to have gained access to it was for them to have been there all the time. When the pond was drawn down the previous fall, these fish had gone into enforced hibernation and had stayed alive, buried in the mud, until the following spring, when they emerged to find a choice meal of trout awaiting them.

When we speak of hibernation and the temperature range at which this annual group movement is reputed to take place,

The Yearly Cycle

I sometimes wonder whether we know, completely, whereof we speak. Mr. Jason Lucas, in his interesting and valuable work, *Lucas on Bass Fishing*, brings out a point concerning hibernation that has been in the back of my mind, although heretofore unexpressed, for a long, long time.

Have you ever noticed that during the fall fishing, when the nights grow cold and water temperatures drop to the low fifties, that you don't catch quite as many bass as you do when the weather is warmer, but have you noticed also that the bass you do catch late in the season average much larger in size than they do at any other time of year? You will find this to be true, season after season. My theory has been—and, believe me, it *is* theory, with only circumstantial evidence to support it—that the larger, adult bass hibernate only for a short time, if at all. I realize that this is heresy and contrary to the teachings of men whose business it is to know about such things, but the fact remains that there is a strong likelihood that all bass do not hibernate. Instead, the big, full-grown fish take up winter quarters in the deeper water and there they stay, swimming about, until spring.

In support of this theory, both I and friends of mine have made unusual catches of large bass during November when the water temperature was in the low forties, ten degrees or more below the mark at which all bass are supposed to hibernate. Mr. Lucas is of the same opinion and he recounts taking excellent catches by fishing well down in the deep water—thirty-five or forty feet—when the air temperature is low enough to freeze the line to the guides of the rod and when ice formed on the side of his boat. Think back, and you will remember hearing or seeing accounts of bass being caught by men who were fishing through the ice for pickerel and perch.

Frankly, I hope that some enterprising and well-insulated ichthyologist takes it upon himself to look into the matter of hibernation more thoroughly. Unquestionably, the smaller

Black Bass

bass do hibernate and, for that matter, probably the majority of the bass do. But I'm still not convinced that all bass hibernate and a great many indications point to the possibility that the big boys—the lunkers—are up and about all winter long in the deep winter holes. I think the matter could do with some investigation.

A bass does not need water over him to stay alive and healthy for a surprisingly long time. If he can be cool and keep his gills moist, he will live out of water for hours. Many times I have had bass live in my creel for as long as six or eight hours after they have been caught. When placed in water, these fish revived quickly and were able to swim about, as good as ever, within a matter of minutes.

As soon as the water warms up to the middle sixties in the spring of each year, spawning activities begin. The fish move into the shallows and the annual reproduction of the species takes place. If gravel or sandy shores are available, there the nests or "reds" are prepared. If not, then the muddy bottoms of the shallows will serve.

Preparation of the nest is sometimes done by an unmated female. She goes ahead with the job in hand while her suitors fight among themselves and vie for her favor between battles. Again, should the pairing process already have been completed, both male and female will join in the preparation of the nest. Usually the male and female are of approximately the same size and the nest is constructed so that it is in circumference from one and a half to two times the length of the fish. All algae, vegetation, and loose silt are fanned away, so that the nest proper is of clean gravel, sand, or firm mud. To get the job done, the fish turns partly on its side and fans away all objectionable matter with vigorous tail strokes. Large pieces of debris either are picked up and carried away or pushed away with the fish's nose.

Bass are prolific spawners, some of the larger females depositing as many as 20,000 eggs, the equivalent of 25 per cent

The Yearly Cycle

of the weight of the fish. Jordan and Everman record an instance of Largemouth spawning near Washington, D.C., in 1892. In one of the rearing ponds, the Fish Commission placed fifteen adult Largemouth Bass prior to the spawning season. Seven or eight of these fish were females. The fish spawned in June and then the adult fish were removed from the pond. At Thanksgiving there were taken out of that pond, by actual count, over 37,000 young bass, each three or four inches long, and approximately five hundred bass that weighed about a half pound each. These fish had received an abundant supply of food but no doubt the larger fish, which were more active feeders, had eaten many of their smaller brothers and sisters. In any event, it is an interesting commentary on the wisdom of stocking a bass pond that already is supplied with even a few pairs of adult breeders.

In deep-water ponds, such as flooded stone quarries, where there are no shallow shores on which to build beds, the bass will construct nests of vegetation such as moss or weed, building on submerged logs or fallen trees so that the nests are perhaps two or three feet under water.

Again, where only a bottom of soft silt is available, nests will be constructed of small twigs and leaves from which the mud and algae have been carefully washed. In short, a bass is a tidy housekeeper and the nest must be clean and spotless. It is not difficult to see bass nests during the spawning season. Just look in the shallows and you will have no trouble locating them, as their scrubbed, clean appearance sets them off in contrast to their surroundings.

The time of the spawning varies according to locality. In Florida and other states of the Deep South, spawning may be completed by the end of February, while in the North the young bass may not be off the nests, in extreme cases, until late June or early July. The general average, however, for most parts of the country is late May or early June. Sixty-seven degrees seems to be the critical temperature for spawn-

Black Bass

ing. Thus, the character of the weather, with its direct influence on water temperatures, will determine the exact time of spawning each year.

There seems to be no set plan to the actual spawning process. Sometimes the female will lay her eggs in the nest, entirely unattended by a male fish. Later on the male shows up and fertilizes the eggs with milt. Again, both male and female can be seen in the nest together, moving about in circles, more or less rapidly, partly tilted over on their sides, the female depositing her eggs and the male fertilizing them as she does so.

Bass eggs, like most fish eggs, are yellow in color. Unlike those of the *Salmo* tribe, they are covered with a glutinous substance which is highly adhesive. For this reason, fish culturists cannot strip the parent fish and handle the eggs the way they do with salmon and trout, as a bass egg will stick to practically anything it happens to touch. Probably for this reason, a female bass will generally lay her eggs in neat rows. Incubation usually takes about eight or ten days, although in abnormally high temperatures the eggs may hatch in as little as seven days and as many as fourteen or fifteen days if the water is colder than it should be. When hatched, the baby bass are almost perfectly formed, quite dark in color and from one quarter to one half an inch long. These tiny fish usually remain in the nest only a few days before taking refuge in the shallows and the weed beds. Rarely are they on the nest as long as a week.

While the eggs are incubating and after the little bass are hatched, the nests are guarded actively by the parent fish. As a rule, the female tires of this police duty rather quickly but the male fish stays on the job during the entire process, taking up his position directly over the nest and keeping the water in motion with his fins. Any intruders are driven away vigorously, and most fish stand not upon the order of their going as a bass is a wicked fighter.

Once the spawning season comes to a close, the Large-

John Alden Knight with his usual equipment for small rivers.

A fine example of North Branch Smallmouth, taken by Ernest Hille on a midget floater.

The Yearly Cycle

mouth chooses his summer quarters. A great many take up residence in comparatively shallow water, selecting living quarters where there is safe cover in the form of logs, brush, weed beds, undercut banks, and such. Some are content to live in the deeper water, cruising in the shallows only during the feeding periods. The majority, however, choose certain localities which they claim as their own and defend against intruders.

When the cool days and frosty nights of October arrive, the fish gradually leave their shallow-water homes and move into deeper water. Then it is that they indulge in an orgy of feeding, taking on extra fat that will keep them sustained during the winter months.

When the water temperatures drop below fifty, feeding slows down and the fish move into winter quarters in the deep backwaters, bays, and coves. There they bury themselves in the mud, or retire to protective cover among logs, stumps, or rocks, and partially suspend animation, their heartbeats slowing down to as little as two or three to the minute. In the smaller lakes and ponds, where the ice may form to considerable depth over the entire surface, there is always the danger of suffocation from lack of oxygen in the water under the ice. Bottom springs, spring runs, feeders, and streams minimize this hazard but it is always there potentially if the winter happens to be an unusually cold one.

As has been noted, the fish remain completely or partially inactive until the ice goes out and the water temperature once more climbs to the vicinity of fifty degrees.

The yearly cycle of the Smallmouth is much the same as that of the Largemouth. He has approximately the same critical temperatures and his spawning dates are about the same, but his habits and his selection of habitat are radically different.

A Smallmouth prefers moving water that is reasonably

cool. Evidently the critical temperature for spawning, sixty-seven degrees, is his preference and he will live in that general temperature band if he can find it. His spawning grounds are chosen either on the shallow "fans" at the tails of the pools in a river, or along the shallow, sandy, or pebbly shores of a river or a pond. Where there is an inlet to a lake that has a cool, even flow, there he will build his nest in the moving waters of the shallows.

The "redding," or preparing, of the nests and the spawning process generally parallel those of the Largemouth, and the Smallmouth is even more vigorous in guarding his nest than is the Largemouth. It makes no difference what size the intruder happens to be, if it comes within the territorial limits of a Smallmouth's nest, depend upon it, there will be an argument unless the interloper retreats in short order.

The spring of 1942 was a cold one in central Pennsylvania with the result that the spawning season was late. Not until mid-June did the beds begin to appear in the shallows. It so happened that I journeyed to the North Branch of the Susquehanna to engage a boat for "opening day." While I was talking to the owner of the boat livery, he remarked on the lateness of the spawning season and also upon the damage that carp do to the bass nests. I expressed the opinion that carp, being vegetarians primarily, received credit for a great deal more damage than they actually do.

"You think so," said the boat owner. "Come along and I'll show you something."

From the vantage point of a high bank we could see the reds in the shallows, almost side by side. Not only that, but we could see a constant state of warfare between the bass and the big river carp that were raiding the nests. The carp of the North Branch are notoriously large, some of them being well up toward the thirty-pound mark and fifteen pounders being quite common. Here and there one of these big fellows would cruise in and raid a bass nest. While he

The Yearly Cycle

was gobbling eggs, the parent bass would smash in savagely from the side, going under the carp in the effort to rip open its belly with the sharp spines of the dorsal fin. Unfortunately, the scales of the carp are too tough for any serious damage to be done, but the bass kept right on trying. Now and again one of the smaller carp would be lifted partly out of the water by the determined charge of a large bass. My ideas about carp damage underwent considerable revision.

Exactly a week later we picked up an excellent catch of bass on opening day in that same "level," as the long pools of the North Branch are called. Without a single exception, both male and female bass had their backs denuded of skin from fighting carp. From nose to dorsal fin the skin and scales were worn completely off so that raw, red muscle was exposed, the injury sometimes being as much as half an inch in width. While the male fish gets most of the credit for defending the nest, in this case both male and female fish had waged long and bitter warfare as was amply attested by their battle scars.

A few years ago, my friend the Fish Warden, while on one of his daily patrols, stopped to look over one of the pools in Lycoming Creek, perhaps six miles from the desk where this is being written. The time was early June and the bass season still some three weeks away. Standing on the high bank above the pool, he noticed a bass bed in the shallow water almost under the bridge. The bed was a small one, as bass nests go, and it was being guarded by one small bass, perhaps ten inches long. While he watched, the bass darted off the nest and drove away an inquisitive sunfish, returning once more to take up his lonely vigil.

About this time a man and two small boys walked out on the bridge, trout rods in hand. Thinking to give the boys a lesson in natural history, the Fish Warden pointed out the bass to the boys and explained to them just what was going on. While they watched, the little bass drove away more small

13

Black Bass

fry, such as chub and sunfish, always returning to his station directly over the bed.

After talking with the trio for a while, the Fish Warden went on about his daily chores. But a warden, to be a good warden, must be observant. As he drove away, automatically he made a mental note of the car that man was driving—a battered Ford of rather ancient vintage. He noted also the license plate which had on it the repetition of two of the numbers.

About two hours later, on his return trip, he stopped again at the bridge, curious to see how the little bass was coming along with his police work. The bed was there all right, but the bass was gone. He waited for about ten minutes but the little bass failed to show up. Then the Fish Warden started out on a search for that battered Ford.

About ten miles upstream, more by good luck than anything else, he spied the ancient Ford where it had been partially hidden from view by a clump of bushes. Down in the pool, out of sight from the road, were the man and the two boys, bait-fishing for trout. The Fish Warden walked down to the water's edge.

When challenged, the man refused to come ashore to be looked over. By that time the Fish Warden was good and mad. He told the man that he'd come ashore willingly and right now or, by God, he'd be brought ashore and he could take his choice. Protesting such persecution of law-abiding citizens, the man waded ashore, dug his license out of his wallet and submitted to a thorough search. No bass. Then the two boys were given the same treatment. Still no bass.

"All right," said the Fish Warden, "we'll look through that car of yours. Come on up and unlock it."

"You got a search warrant?"

"I don't need a search warrant and you know it. Now come on up and unlock that car."

The Yearly Cycle

"I ain't unlockin' that car for nobody. You bothered me enough for one day."

"Listen, buddy," said the Fish Warden. "I carry a good, husky wrecking bar in my car for just such people as you. Now are you going to unlock that car or do I have to pry open the doors and the trunk? Make up your mind."

Grumbling and protesting, the man walked up the bank and unlocked the car. Sure enough, there in the glove pocket was the little ten-inch bass.

"Which one of you caught this bass?" asked the Fish Warden.

"Ain't sayin'," replied the man.

"All right, I'll confiscate all your tackle and take the three of you in."

"Now wait a minute. You can't take them kids' tackle away from them. I caught him."

"O.K. Now get in my car, all of you. We got a date with the Justice of the Peace."

Now this particular Justice happens to be a fisherman. With the bass on his desk before him, he listened as the Fish Warden told him the story. Then, as the saying goes, he "threw the book" at the luckless angler. Maximum fine, full costs, confiscation of tackle, and a recommendation for cancellation of license for two years attached to the report to be sent in to headquarters. Not only that but, with two wide-eyed youngsters listening to every word, the Justice gave the fellow a verbal going-over that he wouldn't forget in a hurry. Then, to top off the entire matter, the Fish Warden declined to furnish transportation back to the battered Ford, standing in the bushes fourteen miles upstream. Without doubt, that fellow will think twice before he catches another bass off a spawning bed during the closed season. Incidentally, that bass proved, upon examination, to be a male fish.

Generally speaking, bass do not feed while they are on the spawning beds. Unscrupulous fishermen have learned that the parent fish will pick up baits that have been dropped directly in the nest, but they pick them up to remove them from the nest, not to eat them. That was how the man caught the little bass under the bridge. He dropped directly in the bed a hook that was baited with a big nightwalker. Then when the little bass picked it up to carry it to one side, he jerked the hook home.

In early May of 1944, two friends and I journeyed to Currituck Sound, South Carolina, to fish for brackish water bass. The spawning season was late that year and many bass were still on the beds when we arrived. Experimentally, we cast our bass bugs over the beds but the bass ignored them.

We had no intention of keeping any fish thus caught, regardless of size. We merely wished to see what would happen. As I say, the bass refused our best offerings. Judged by the standards of that country, we had poor fishing even though we did manage to hook, land, and release one hundred and seventeen bass in a single day. One of my friends returned to the same fishing grounds about three weeks later and enjoyed superlative fishing.

Like the Largemouth fry, the baby Smallmouth are almost fully developed fish when hatched. I've seen them by the thousands in the shallows along the banks of the upper Delaware—tiny little black things, taking cover among the stones and pebbles.

One July, my son and I, being curious as to the productivity of that natural bass hatchery, the West Branch of the Delaware River, undertook to do a "fry count." We did this by selecting sample strips of shoal water, of known length. Proceeding carefully and slowly, we counted the fry in these strips, quite a chore in view of the fact that each rock and pebble must be investigated and due allowance made for duplication. The type of shore line also needed to be taken into account as some sections of the stream hold many more bass than do other less favorable types. This

The Yearly Cycle

job done and our counts made, we sat down and did some simple arithmetic. Then, as a factor of safety, we divided our total by two and considered that to be approximately the correct result. According to this method, the upper Delaware produced that year about half a million fry per mile.

There seems to be some confusion and disagreement as to the manner in which infant bass find their collective way from the nest to the safe cover of the shallows and the weed beds, there to grow to maturity if they can. Some accounts state that the parent fish conduct the youngsters on a personally chaperoned tour from nest to shallows, both parents being in attendance. These accounts do not state specifically that the recorder thereof actually has witnessed such excursions. They merely set it down as a fact and let it go at that.

Other writers give all credit for child rearing to the male fish. Unquestionably, the male bass is the more vigilant and the more faithful of the two in the protection of the progeny. But the battle scars that result from the annual bass-carp warfare in the North Branch of the Susquehanna point strongly to the fact that the female does lend a helping hand in the care of the young.

Lacking evidence to the contrary, it is my belief that small bass leave the nest gradually, as individuals, the more active fish first, followed by the less precocious until, finally, all have set out on their own or have been devoured by larger fish. This is not true of other varieties of fry. I have seen long parades of baby catfish, black as your hat and none of them an inch long, playing "follow the leader" in the shallows, the nose of one almost touching the tail of the next. Their pace was dignified and unhurried and evidently they were as dependent, one upon the other, as so many sheep in a herded flock. But baby bass don't behave that way. With them it's more of a case of every man for himself. Until I witness factual evidence to the contrary, I will continue

Black Bass

to believe that they leave the nest individually, when they happen to feel like making a change.

Spawning season at an end, the adult Smallmouth do not tarry long near the spawning beds. Their preference for summer quarters is a rocky shore line with plenty of cover and a ready supply of moving, cool water. These requirements are not necessarily confined to bass rivers. In the larger lakes, wind action keeps the water pretty much in motion most of the time. Consider, for instance, Georgian Bay on the north shore of Lake Ontario—a famous place for bass. The bay is dotted with islands of all sizes and between them are the channels or "thoroughfares." Through experience the guides have found that there is nearly always a concentration of Smallmouth where one of these thoroughfare currents spends itself against the open waters of the bay. In the smaller lakes the Smallmouth must content themselves with inlet flow, "spring holes," or the most comfortable temperature layer of the thermocline (we'll talk about that later), but in the larger lakes circumstances are more generous.

In a bass river, particularly in a large one, the same general rules obtain. Moving water, sixty-seven degrees or thereabouts if possible, on a rocky shore line that is deep enough to afford adequate cover—that's where you will find your largest concentrations. To be sure, you will find some Smallmouth scattered about in all parts of a good bass river. Sometimes, probably because of an unusual food condition, you will find them in the most surprising places, but mostly the "hot spots" are the moderately deep, rocky shore lines where the flow is steady and cool. Remember that and your days after Smallmouth will be happy ones; forget it, and you are apt to spend a great deal of time fishing water that is comparatively barren.

As the season progresses, the Smallmouth may or may not continue to live in their chosen locations that were satisfactory during late June and early July. Water conditions and temperatures play an important part in this decision.

The Yearly Cycle

Should the water level, in either a river or lake, become abnormally low, cover that was satisfactory in the early season becomes unsafe and too warm for comfort. Thus, the fish move out and retire to the deeper water. Should floods or high water levels occur, as they sometimes do, there will be a complete redistribution of the bass population. But if conditions remain anywhere near normal, the Smallmouth will stay in their chosen homes until the cool fall days arrive. Then, gradually, they go to the deeper waters in preparation for the coming winter hibernation period.

For reasons best known to the ichthyologists, little if any work has been done on the migrations of Smallmouth bass—and Largemouth, too, for that matter. That may be an unfair statement. I hope not. But search as I will, I can find no written data or information on bass migrations. The fact remains, however, that these migrations do occur. Lacking positive evidence on the subject, I must be content with the circumstantial, but this is strong enough to be quite conclusive.

Consider, in point, the Delaware River. People tell me that I talk too much about the Delaware. Well, maybe I do. It is a pretty good river to talk about as it is doubtful that there is a better Smallmouth river anywhere in this world than the Delaware. It has everything that a Smallmouth could want. Length, size, character of water, rate of drop, food supply, temperature—everything is perfect. For nearly thirty years I have fished its friendly waters each summer and it has fallen to my lot to catch many thousands of Smallmouth from its generous pools and runs. Being, in my modest but sincere opinion, the perfect bass river, it is not unreasonable to assume that what holds good in the Delaware should also be true of other good bass rivers.

My son, Dick, and I prefer to wade for our Smallmouth, if possible. Thus, we spend a great deal of time in the headwaters of the Delaware—the West Branch between the towns

Black Bass

of Deposit and Hancock, New York State. The West Branch is a friendly river, ideal for wading and fishing with a fly rod. In the ten miles of stream that we fish, year after year, the fishing has remained universally good. It is not uncommon for us to hook and land seventy-five or a hundred bass on the two rods in a single day. I hasten to add that we kill very few fish—only enough to give us what we, personally, want to eat. The rest are released, a little tired, perhaps, after the fight to the net but otherwise unharmed and, we hope, a little wiser in the ways of men with fly rods.

In the twenty-nine summers that I have fished these same waters, I have noted one inescapable fact. Year after year, the *average* size of the fish that we catch remains the same. Not that we don't have interesting and, all too often, unsuccessful entanglements with large bass in these waters. We do. But these engagements are, outstandingly, the exceptions rather than the rule. Every year our *average*—and I put the word in italics to emphasize it—remains at about twelve inches in length and three quarters of a pound in weight. In other words, we catch a great many two-year-old bass. That is in the ten miles of good water between Hancock and Deposit.

All right, let's go downstream a mere matter of five miles. That puts us below the junction of the East Branch and the West Branch where, naturally, the river is considerably larger. Immediately the normal catch is stepped up another inch or so and the *average* fish is well over a foot long. I think fourteen inches would be a fair estimate.

Now—let's take a long jump down to the big river around Mast Hope or Narrowsburg or Delaware Water Gap. Here you are fishing for adult Smallmouth—fish that will run from two to four pounds. To be sure, there are small bass in these waters also, but, conversely, *these* are the exception in the lower river; just the reverse of conditions in the West Branch.

Obviously, in view of the fact that these size-to-water ratios continue to remain constant year after year, the Smallmouth,

The Yearly Cycle

as they grow, move down to waters of a size commensurate with their bulk. Since the two-year-olds of one fall are not there, in their state of advanced growth, the following summer they must, of necessity, move downstream. There's no place else for them to go.

This same condition is true of the North Branch of the Susquehanna River. Dick and I have fished these waters from headwaters, so small that I can toss a stone easily from bank to bank with my left hand, to the big water some twenty miles above Wilkes-Barre, Pennsylvania. The ratios are the same—small water, small fish; big water, big fish. Lacking the theory of either fall or spring migration, there is no other way to account for it. Thus, the inescapable conclusion must be that the bass, as they grow, move down into larger waters which are more commensurate with their added stature; this, I suppose, is a migration of sorts.

When the fall feeding spree is over, and the cold days of winter place ice in the shallows, most of the Smallmouth go into winter hibernation. Here they remain, semicomatose, until the kindly sun of mild spring days warms the water and stirs them from their long winter's sleep. Four to six weeks of increasing activity and feeding bring them once more to the spawning season. So goes the yearly cycle.

CHAPTER 2

Characteristics and Behavior of Bass

~~~~~~

FROM THE STANDPOINT of characteristics and general behavior in response to certain stimuli, Smallmouth Bass and Largemouth Bass are pretty much alike. Oh, they have their differences and their little quirks and mannerisms but, by and large, they are quite similar in their actions.

In the first place, bass are not shy, that is, in the sense that trout are shy. They are wary and smart (as fish go), but they do not indulge in distracted, unreasoning spasms of fright as do the members of the *Salmo* family. When you alarm a trout, he rushes away madly, sometimes bumping into things or going the wrong direction, in the frantic effort to find safe cover or deep water. Not so a bass. To be sure, he moves away at a good rate of speed if you happen to get too close to him, but his retreat is well ordered and he doesn't scurry.

Some years ago, probably around 1936, I sat on a high bank above the Delaware and watched a man fish his way up through the pool. The water was low and clear at the time and I could see everything that happened below me. As I watched, something attracted my attention upstream from the fisherman. To my surprise, I saw the unmistakable wake of a large fish as it moved away from the shore line. Its prog-

Characteristics and Behavior of Bass

ress was leisurely but steady, and it swam directly across the river, then downstream past where I was sitting, bypassing the angler. As the fish passed my point of vantage I could see quite clearly that it was a bass of probably three or four pounds. It kept on going downstream until it was lost to view.

As I sat there watching, an even dozen of those big fish left the deeper shore line, swam around the fisherman, and disappeared downstream. They weren't alarmed, they weren't in fear of their lives; they merely were wise and wary enough to wish to keep plenty of distance between themselves and this noisy creature who made so much fuss kicking his rough shoes against the rocks of the river bottom. Not one of them allowed the man to approach within seventy-five yards of its resting station without moving. And, incidentally, who says there are no large bass in the upper Delaware? Not a single one of those fish weighed less than three pounds and most of them were more likely to be four pounds or better.

Those fish, of course, were Smallmouth Bass. I have never seen Largemouth behave in this way. Usually they merely hide under the cover that they have chosen for their homes and there they stay unless you prod them out with an oar or a stick. Even then their flight is well ordered and sure, and they seem to know exactly where they are going.

Bass seem to differentiate between what might be called friendly and unfriendly noises. The bump of a paddle or an oar against the side of your boat often will raise the devil with your fishing for quite a distance. Loud talk, laughter, and shouting will do the same. Don't think for a minute because a noise originates outside the water that the fish can't hear it or, to be more accurate, *feel* it. The nerve ends of the auditory or vibration-conscious nervous system terminate along the lateral line on each side, and he is extremely sensitive to vibrations of every kind. Shouts and laughter are vibrations, and he can feel them quite plainly. Noisy oarlocks on a boat come under the same category. We always pack loose oarlocks with bits of rope, cut from the end of the anchor line. This, when wet, makes a snug fit and will render the loosest oarlock absolutely silent in operation.

As for the friendly noises, I suppose that the one with which we are mostly concerned is the splash that is made by a leaping fish. I may be wrong about this, but it always has seemed to me that the jump and resultant splash of a hooked bass does not necessarily alarm other bass in that general vicinity. The noise and commotion excite them and often attract them to the scene of conflict, but I've never found that they consider this sort of noise as a warning. Probably the reason is that a bass is apt to make a pretty loud splash when he takes food from the surface, such as a moving or fluttering insect. Thus, the noise may be regarded as being indicative of the presence of food, and where there is one tasty morsel, there is apt to be more. So the other fish rally round to see what goes on.

Not infrequently a bass will "miss his strike" at a surface lure. I don't believe for one minute that a bass ever "misses" latching onto a surface lure if he really wants it. Instead, for one reason or another, he changes his mind at the last minute and the splash that usually accompanies a "missed strike" is caused by the hurried turn he makes at the surface to return to his resting station. As often as not, on the very next cast to that same spot that same bass or one just like him will rise and take the lure solidly.

Dick and I have a place in the Delaware that we call the "Bass Mine." This stretch of water is perhaps a hundred yards long and about fifty or sixty feet wide. It is not deep—three or four feet at most—but the bottom is littered with big boulders that make wading a sore trial. For some reason this area always holds a liberal supply of big bass, at least they

Characteristics and Behavior of Bass

are big for the Delaware. Instead of averaging the usual twelve inches, these fish run much heavier. It is uncommon to hook a bass in these waters that weighs less than two pounds. These roughnecks, living as they do in cold, moving water, are rugged citizens and they give a good account of themselves when hooked. But regardless of how much fuss they make while we are fighting them in to the net, their brothers and sisters don't seem to mind in the least. I have stood in one spot and hooked, played, and landed nine or ten of these fish in the course of an hour. The last one always takes the lure just as readily and with as little reserve as did the first. On the other hand, let us make the mistake of wading carelessly and scraping hobnails on the river bottom and we might just as well have stayed home for all the big bass we'll take from the Bass Mine.

Another thing that convinces me that bass do not become alarmed over the rumpus that is made by a hooked fish is the frequency with which other bass will follow that fish in, sometimes within rod length. If they were frightened by this unusual commotion, the last thing they would do would be to follow the source of the noise around, evidently to see what is going on.

Just as noises are divided into friendly and unfriendly categories, so are motions. Generally speaking, slow, smoothly made motions will not alarm fish, whereas fast, suddenly made motions will cause considerable concern. Tree branches, waving in the wind over a stream or the edge of a lake, are normal everyday motions to which fish become accustomed. Probably for this reason the smooth, rhythmic movement of a rod tip, which a great many fish certainly can see, causes no alarm. The slow movement of a canoe paddle in the water does no harm. But here's one thing that does. A good many men have the amateurish habit of paddling first on one side, then on the other. When changing sides, the usual custom is to swing the paddle up in a high arc overhead so that drops of water will not be thrown into the boat. In the first place, that's not the way to paddle a canoe or a boat. When you are fishing a shore line, keep your paddle in the water and feather it between strokes. Make your strokes smooth and unhurried and don't bump the gunwale. And *don't* change sides, throwing drops of water about and flashing your paddle in the sun with a hurried, unnatural motion. If you are careful about these things, you will enjoy better fishing.

The scientists tell us that a bass is nearsighted, at least some of them do. Every time I read such a statement, I conclude that that particular scientist hasn't done very much bass fishing. Shucks, a bass can see you just as far off as you can see him. He doesn't spend his time gazing into the misty green vastness of the waters around him, thereby dimming his capacity for seeing long distances. Instead, a great deal of his time is spent watching the surface for food and the air above him for possible threats of danger. Take a look at a bass sometime with this in mind and notice how his eyes are placed. He has a very wide range of vision, particularly above him. Depend upon it, if you can see any objects that lie beneath the surface of the water, a fish that lies beside those objects can see you, so guide yourself accordingly. Yes, I've read all about a fish's "window" and I've studied light refraction and so on. Those things are nice to discuss and theorize about when you haven't much else to do. But a better way is to put on a pair of polaroid glasses, to remove the "glint" from the surface of the water, and then find out for yourself how far away you have to be before you become invisible to a fish. It's farther than you think, at least it is if you happen to belong to the "fish window" school of thought.

As to color discrimination, I'm content to take the scientists' word on that. They say that a fish has an acute sense of color perception. Certainly the preference that bass show now and then for lures of a certain color over lures of other

Average bass are larger in the fall of the year than in the summer.

Dick landing a small one from the "Goldfish Bowl" in the upper Delaware.

Characteristics and Behavior of Bass

colors, although identical in design and action, is sufficient proof that bass can distinguish one color from another. After all, this book is primarily for fishermen and if we know that a bass can tell a red plug from a blue one or a yellow one, that should be enough for the purpose in hand.

As to whether or not a bass can hear, it seems to be quite clearly established that he can. He has ears. To be sure, they are tiny, undeveloped things, but his vibration-perception apparatus is as sensitive as any radar set. He can run down and catch his prey in jet-black darkness, merely by following the vibrations it makes as it passes through the water ahead of him. It is for this reason that a black plug or a black fly makes a good lure on a dark night when literally you can't see your hand when it is held directly before your face. I don't think that the bass actually can see the lure—there is less light down where he is than where you are—but he hits it with unerring certainty, largely by following its vibrations as it moves through the water. This same sensitivity to vibrations serves him as a sense of hearing, and the whole assembly is far more acute and finely tuned than anything we humans have.

In the matter of taste and smell—well, that is subject to some discussion. Surely some fish have those senses. Consider fish spawn, for instance. Fish eggs on the bottom of a stream look much like little round pebbles. Yet other fish will gobble up every last one of them. They must have some way to distinguish eggs from pebbles other than eyesight alone.

Then, too, fish are attracted by high-smelling odors. There used to be an old fellow who had phenomenal success at bass fishing in Tuxedo Lake, New York State. He would use the same bait as his companions but almost invariably his luck was better and his catches larger, even when fishing from the same boat as his less fortunate cronies. All of them knew that when this man baited his hook, he would turn his back, go through some mysterious motions, and then hurriedly throw the bait into the water. At last, one fatal day he left his coat on the dock and one of his coanglers went through his pockets. There he found a tube of rubber cement. That was before the days of modern commercial solvents and rubber cement was held in solution by carbon disulphide, which, as you know, smells like badly spoiled eggs. The old fellow had merely been squeezing a small quantity of this cement onto each bait and then capping the tube and putting it back in his pocket. Evidently the fish were attracted by the carbon disulphide as the old man surely produced plenty of bass from that lake.

Another fellow up Nipigon way carried a bottle of sinister brown liquid which he vowed attracted fish from far and near. The stuff smelled to high heaven, even out in the open air, but he used it religiously when he and my friend went fishing. All of the other guides in that area tried by every means they could contrive to discover the ingredients that went into that mixture, but without success. It must be admitted, however, that the awful-smelling mess did seem to attract fish.

When my friend's vacation came to an end, he and his old guide were standing at the station, waiting for the train. In a friendly burst of confidence, the guide said to him, "You want to know what's in that bottle? Well, I'll tell yuh, but don't let on to nobody—extract of beaver balls."

If you will browse through the classified advertising of the outdoor magazines, you will find advertisements offering for sale various guaranteed baits for carp, catfish, and such. Almost without exception, these are concocted with a liberal application of one or more of the essential oils—anise, pennyroyal, and so on. And, strangely enough, they seem to catch fish.

Yes, I think a bass has a sense of taste or smell, at least he has taste perceptions. They probably differ from ours but the result is the same.

Characteristics and Behavior of Bass

The physicists tell us that each substance or material is made up of molecules that have their own particular sorts of vibrations. It may be that this is the guiding factor that enables a fish to distinguish the edible from the inedible. Consider for a moment the presence of blood in the water. Anyone who has done deep-sea angling knows how blood will attract sharks. Just let a fish be hooked deeply so that he is bleeding freely and your chances of getting him into the boat intact are poor indeed. Sharks come from all directions at the first sign of blood. Now, blood from a bleeding fish surely is confined to the area in which that fish swims. It is unlikely that the actual odor of blood extends itself very far from that immediate vicinity. Yet the sharks, being predatory scavengers and having their own radar sets tuned up to be able to detect such things, pick up these minute vibrations that the blood molecules send out, and come hurrying in, unerringly, for the feast.

While the nervous system of a bass is far more finely tuned than ours for some purposes, it is surprisingly lacking in other respects. Although the bass is acutely conscious of vibrations, actual hearing, as we understand it, is comparatively undeveloped. By the same token, even though a bass has a well-developed sense of touch, there is little evidence that he has any sense of pain. In witness of this lack of capacity for suffering, there are countless incidents which testify that injury actually does not *hurt* a bass, in the sense that injury hurts us, thereby causing him to suffer.

Consider again the self-inflicted wounds of the North Branch bass, when they wage their annual warfare with the carp on the spawning beds. Some of these wounds are half an inch wide and several inches long, exposing red, raw flesh. Yet the bass keep on fighting just so long as the carp continue to invade the spawning grounds. Time after time, they rub those raw, red abrasions anew against the iron-clad, scaly hides of their adversaries. If pain existed, as we know it,

Black Bass

it is doubtful that they could continue with the fight, even though they wished to do so.

When Dick was a little fellow, too small to handle a bass-bug rod, he used to fish with helgramites. One day in the lower Delaware he landed a bass of about a pound. When he picked it up to extract the hook, he noticed a piece of black fishing line hanging from its mouth. Investigation showed that the line was fastened to a number-one bait hook and this was imbedded solidly in its throat, about midway between its mouth and its stomach, a partially digested helgramite still fastened to the bend of the hook. While this assembly certainly must have been uncomfortable, it did not prevent his feeding, as his stomach was partially full of various sorts of food. Meanwhile, to find this food, he had been trailing over the rocks of the river bottom about five feet of stout line which must, now and then, have caught between the stones and given the hook a good, solid tug.

In the upper Delaware there is a deep little saucer of a "hole" located near the bank at the base of a long, shallow "flat." Being a natural concentration spot for the fish in that area, we can, when the going gets tough, pick up a mess of fish from this spot. For convenience, we call it the Goldfish Bowl.

One evening, just about dusk, after a rather unsuccessful day's fishing, I waded over to the Goldfish Bowl to see if I could round out a mess by adding just one more bass. My first cast was met by a heavy strike, and the bass and I settled down to work. He proved to be an active fish, dashing back and forth and jumping repeatedly. During the course of the battle, he managed to wedge one of the knots of my heavy leader between two rocks in the shallower water. This gave him the downhill pull he needed and he departed from there right then.

Expecting to find my bass bug gone the way of all good bass bugs, I reeled in my line and waded over to disengage

Characteristics and Behavior of Bass

my leader. To my surprise, the bug was still there, and wedged into the bend of the hook was the complete maxillary shield of a fairly large bass. The pull of the hook had ripped down through the light membrane throughout the length of the shield and, when its wide end had jammed in in the bend of the hook, the fastening near the nose of the fish had torn free.

Bemoaning my luck, I waded back across the flat and sat down on the bank to dress out my catch. This done, the idea occurred to me that the Goldfish Bowl would have had time to quiet down, so I waded back within casting range and placed the bug over next to the far bank. As before, it was taken solidly, almost as soon as it struck the water. This time I was more fortunate and managed to land the fish—a very respectable three pounder. It being nearly dark by that time, I made my way back to the car with the bass still in my net. Then in the headlights, I took the bass from the net to disengage the hook. Sure enough, one maxillary shield was gone, freshly torn away, with the place where it had been still raw and bleeding. Evidently pain hadn't bothered that bass very much.

As I say, it is dubious that injury actually hurts a bass. I've caught them with raw, festered wounds on their sides; with badly corroded hooks in their gills and their throats; with bass plugs hanging to their gill covers, the hooks partially rotted free and the gill covers badly the worse for wear. Should any of these fish have had any sense of actual pain, the probabilities are that they would not have been feeding actively until their injuries were on the mend.

For some reason, not clear to me, a great many bass fishermen have trouble now and then distinguishing Largemouth Bass from Smallmouth Bass. Personally, I don't think a Largemouth looks any more like a Smallmouth than an Irishman looks like a Chinaman. But for those who do have trouble and want to be sure, here are some easy rules.

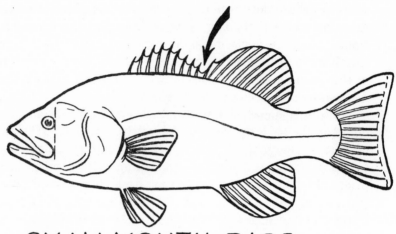

SMALLMOUTH BASS

LARGEMOUTH BASS

*Two easy ways of determining the species of a bass—the **maxillary** shield and the notch in the dorsal fin.*

Characteristics and Behavior of Bass

With the Smallmouth, the end of the upper jawbone or maxillary shield does not extend behind a vertical line dropped from the back of the eye. With the Largemouth, this jawbone or shield extends noticeably behind such a line. The cheek scales of a Smallmouth are arranged in twelve or more rows, usually about fourteen, whereas the cheek scales of the Largemouth are set in from nine to twelve rows. The dorsal fin of a Smallmouth is not deeply notched, while the dorsal fin of a Largemouth is so deeply notched as to give the appearance of being divided. The Smallmouth has small scales on the bases of the membranes of the dorsal and anal fins and the Largemouth lacks such scales. In addition, the Largemouth generally is more silvery in color and the lateral line stands out in sharp contrast. Generally the Smallmouth is built along trim lines but the Largemouth, if he is well fed, is apt to take on a pot belly like that of a portly alderman.

There is usually some difference in the manner in which a Smallmouth takes a lure and the way a Largemouth takes one. Generally a Smallmouth takes a lure rather casually. A surface lure, more often than not, he takes with a tip-up rise and a swirl. If he happens to be a shore-line bass, usually he will turn with the lure in his mouth and start back to his feeding station. But if he is a cruiser, out in deep water or feeding across the shallow fan of a pool, frequently he is content to capture the lure, not moving after he takes it, but merely holding it in his mouth.

Sometime when you visit a hatchery, get one of the attendants to supply you with a handful of fish food. First, throw a few pieces into one of the rearing ponds that hold trout and note how the food is taken with a rush and a graceful turn, the fish rarely remaining at the spot where the food was taken. Then go over to the Smallmouth pond and throw in some food. Of course it is taken with a rush; competition is keen in a rearing pond. But note the very high percentage of fish who rush in, grab the food, and then sit right there while they consume it.

All right—now go to the Largemouth pond and throw in some food. Some of them behave just as the Smallmouth do, consuming the food on the spot without moving, but a great many of them will rush in, grab the food, and then turn to go back from where they came. These characteristic feeding mannerisms hold good in a stream or a lake, just as they do in a hatchery pond.

Many fishermen "low rate" the Largemouth, claiming that he is far inferior to the Smallmouth. Well, every man to his taste, but I always suspect a man's knowledge of bass and bass fishing when he makes that statement. The honest, enthusiastic, unrestrained, whole-hearted way that a Largemouth wallops a surface lure has endeared him forever to my heart. Nothing that the Smallmouth does can compare with the unannounced, explosive strike of his big-mouthed cousin. It's one of the really great thrills that Mother Nature has to offer us.

Once in a while you will find a Smallmouth who will make your hair stand on end when he hits a surface lure, but these are the exceptions. One day a friend and I were fishing one of the pools of the North Branch of the Susquehanna. It was the first time I had fished for bass with him. He never had fished a bass bug in the daytime and he was under the impression that the only time that these lures were effective was after dark. That's right, so help me; as recently as 1939 that was the common belief in central Pennsylvania. Folks looked at me as though I were crazy when I said I fished bass bugs in the daytime as I didn't care much for night fishing.

Accordingly, when I went over to visit my friend at his camp, he insisted upon leaving his rod in his tent. He'd row the boat and watch. Later he confessed that when we started out he didn't expect me to raise a single bass.

Characteristics and Behavior of Bass

The pool that we fished is about a mile long and at its lower end it pulls down into a narrow channel or "draw" which terminates in a truly vicious stretch of rapids. In this "draw" the river flows, fast, deep, and smooth, over a jumble of huge, round boulders, and it is a notorious place for big bass. The rapid current keeps the water fresh, right up to the steep shoreline.

We had taken some fair bass—two to three pounds—and were well down in the draw. The bug, when cast to the shoreline, would be whisked out and away quite rapidly. I was handling quite a long line so that the bug would have a chance to play both at the shoreline and over the tops of the boulders as the current swung it to a position below me.

There was one particularly likely looking spot along the shore and I asked my friend to hold the boat near there while I cast and recast over it. At last, despairing of raising a fish, I allowed the bug to make its way erratically across the current. When it was at least twenty feet from shore, a whopping big bass burst from the pocket near shore that I had been fishing. For the full twenty feet, at lightening speed, he fairly skimmed over the surface, half out of the water for the entire distance, and fell on that bass bug like a wolf. As I say, he was a big devil, hard and very strong, and we had quite a contest there in that heavy flow until I managed to lead him up into the deeper, slower water. There we fought it out and he came back to camp with us on the stringer, all four pounds of him. I have seen Largemouth do this sort of thing a good many times but that is one of the very few times I have had a Smallmouth do it for me. Needless to say, my friend is now a confirmed *daylight* bass-bug fisherman.

For the life of me, I can't understand how anybody can doubt that a bass is endowed with an inherent pugnacity that is second to none in fresh water. He is a wicked and a courageous fighter, as is amply attested by the battle scars of those North Branch bass during the spawning season when

35

Black Bass

they take on fish ten times their weight. With his dorsal fin he can slash open the belly of a pickerel, killing it almost immediately. I think a bass enjoys a fight and is always ready for one.

One day, while fishing the Chenango River of New York State, I had hooked a river chub about a foot long. As I brought the chub in, out of nowhere came a small bass, at the very most not over seven inches long. Without hesitation, he darted through the water and gave that unlucky chub a good, solid bump on the side with his nose. Curious to see what would happen, I gave the chub some line and let him swim around in front of me. Time after time that little bass attacked. From what I could see, he made no attempt to bite the chub. Instead, he rammed it with his nose and twice he went under it, inflicting cuts with his dorsal fin. It was as complete an example of unprovoked cussedness as I ever saw.

Almost every bass fisherman has hooked bass on plugs that are as large as, or larger than, the fish itself. What would prompt a little bass to strike another fish, or what he takes for a fish, that is larger than he is if it isn't pugnacity? I have always felt that this very characteristic is responsible for the fact that we can catch bass on large plugs. They are too big for the bass to eat but they are not too big to kill.

The black bass has a fighting style all his own. He hasn't the "Fancy Dan" form that is typical of most of the *Salmo* tribe, and he isn't flashy, except with certain rare exceptions. Mostly, his battle against rod and reel consists of determined, brute-strength tactics, with now and then a jump for liberty. But he will fight it out, right down to his last ounce of strength, and when, at long last, he does turn on his side, you know that you have had a war on your hands. Dr. James A. Henshall, in his famous book, *Book of the Black Bass*, coined a phrase about the black bass. "Inch for inch, and pound for pound, the gamest fish that swims." That's what he thought about it. He should have added the words "in fresh water"

Characteristics and Behavior of Bass

to that memorable line if he intended to convey the idea of strength for weight. But I don't think that the good doctor had exactly that in mind. He knew, just as well as you and I do, that there are stronger fish in salt water than the black bass. What he probably intended was to convey the idea that a black bass is a gentleman, a sportsman, and a worthy antagonist who will give you everything he has and ask no quarter; that he will take an artificial lure cleanly and readily, and that he will increase greatly your pleasure in the outdoors if you give him the chance to do so by fishing for him with proper tackle.

From time to time you hear and read considerable discussion about the relative fighting abilities of the Smallmouth and the Largemouth. For some reason, most folks seem to be under the impression that the Smallmouth, pound for pound, is a more able scrapper than the Largemouth. I never have been able to convince myself that this is true. In this connection, it must be remembered that the Largemouth is quite contented in warm, sluggish water in which a Smallmouth would be miserable. Conversely, a Smallmouth prefers, in a river, "live water," and he makes his home on rocky bottoms where there is a ready supply of fresh, cool, well-aerated flow. When you hook him in such surroundings, remember that he has the current to help him, whereas the Largemouth wages his battle in water that is comparatively motionless. That makes a great difference. Dr. Henshall maintains, and so does Jason Lucas, that Smallmouth and Largemouth *that live in the same water* put about the same degree of intensity, effort, resistance, fight—call it what you will—into their battles to the net. I'm inclined to agree with Dr. Henshall and Mr. Lucas.

But I think the matter goes a little deeper than that. The Smallmouth and the Largemouth have different styles of fighting, just as two pugilists differ somewhat in their methods of attack and defense. This difference is difficult to put into

37

Black Bass

words. It might be summed up this way—the Smallmouth is faster and flashier in his runs, but the Largemouth has more bulldog determination and tenacity.

Some years ago, George Donovan and I were fishing a bass bug for Smallmouth in the Clyde River of Vermont. I was handling the fly rod at the time and George was rowing. We were fishing a deep-water shore line when an able bass came tearing in from the side, dorsal fin out of the water, and fell on the bug with a heart-warming smash. That, of itself, was unusual. George pulled the boat away from shore and the bass and I fought it out in deep water. He was the flashiest bass I ever saw. His runs were lightning fast and his jumps were something to behold. No straight-up-and-down jumps for that boy—he carried on like a salmon, often turning complete somersaults in the air. During one of his runs he left the water and his speed, no doubt helped by the spring tension of the rod, carried him twelve or fifteen feet through the air before he struck the water again, nose first, without any reduction in speed as he completed his run. With all of the thousands of bass that I have been lucky enough to catch, I've never seen one put on a performance like that. Needless to say, no Largemouth ever has approached it.

On the other hand, the Largemouth has a trick that I have not seen displayed by the Smallmouth. When a Smallmouth decides to jump, in his effort to rid himself of the hook, he will work his way up toward the surface, using only the last two or three feet to give him his running start that will carry him up into the air. Not so a Largemouth. When one of these, particularly a big one, sounds, right down to the bottom, in twelve or fourteen feet of water, look out! Often that is the danger signal. Starting at the bottom, he will come straight up at top speed and his rush is apt to carry him two or three feet clear of the water. There he seems to hang for a moment while he shakes and tosses his head from side to side. It's a lovely thing to watch, particularly during

Characteristics and Behavior of Bass

the sunset hours when the golden glow is reflected from his shiny side.

Many years ago, when we lived in Florida, I spent a great deal of time fishing for bass in the lakes and rivers of that state. We had acquired a small, skeleton trailer, built on the front axle assembly of a Model T Ford, and thereupon we toted a light, square-ended, flat-bottomed fishing boat. We specialized in fishing new lakes, using a topographic map to guide us, and rarely fishing the same lake twice. In so doing, we learned two basic truths. Every lake in Florida holds bass (at least, we have yet to find one that doesn't, and we fished hundreds of them) and, more important for our purposes here, the character of the lake and the temperature of the water have a great deal of bearing on the fighting qualities, and the taste, of the bass the lake contains.

A great many of the lakes we fished were flat bottomed, shallow, muddy affairs that ran high temperatures under Florida's summer sun. All of them teemed with fish and animal life and the bass they held were big, fat, pot-bellied bruisers, lazy almost to the point of lethargy. Now and again, however, we would find a spring-fed lake, with white sand bottom instead of mud, and crystal-clear water. The bass from such a lake were something else again—trim, husky, active fish that fought like demons. I remember a six pounder that I hooked in such a lake over back of Clermont one hot summer afternoon. By my wrist watch, it took me over twenty minutes to get him into the boat, this despite the fact that the plug was in his mouth so that he could not close his jaws. You won't find many Smallmouth, regardless of size, that will fight rod and reel for twenty minutes. Yet this bass was a Florida Largemouth and these, as you know, are not supposed to be such-a-much as fighters when compared to the average Smallmouth.

As I say, the character of the fight—the fighting style—of the two varieties differs. In the North Branch of the Susque-

Black Bass

hanna River of Pennsylvania there is a scattering of Large-mouth although this stream is primarily populated by Small-mouth. Naturally, we hook one of these Largemouth every once in a while. Not once but many times I have remarked to my companion that I have hooked a Largemouth before I have had a look at the fish I was fighting. It isn't that the strike is less solid or the battle less energetic and exciting. It is merely "different" and I can't, for the life of me, find the words to tell you why.

It is doubtful that the dispute as to the relative fighting qualities and general all-round worth of the two varieties ever will be decided. But what of it? Both are splendid game fish —and who expects agreement among fishermen, anyway?

CHAPTER 3

Food and Feeding
Habits of Bass

FROM THE TIME that they are hatched from the eggs on the spawning beds, bass are carnivorous. At least we can find no record that bass, in their wild state and natural habitat, ever indulge their appetites with anything other than fresh meat of one sort or another. As soon as they leave the nests, they begin to feed on minute crustacea that they find in the water about them. As they grow, this diet is widened to include small insect larvae and tiny fish. Gradually the scope of their menu is extended until at maturity a bass will sample almost anything that lives, moves, looks even remotely edible, and is not too big to swallow. Once in a while a bass will out-guess himself as to his swallowing capacity. This results in a stalemate, and swallower and swallowee are found washed up in the shallows, hopelessly interlocked and both dead, ready to have their picture taken for publication in one of the outdoor magazines.

While the variety of small creatures on which a bass feeds is quite extensive, he seems to have his preferences. From my own observations, there evidently is no set plan whereby certain types of food are favored over other types as the season progresses. There are, however, some generalities, but even these are vague at best and subject to complete reversals now and then. Why bass go in for their evident inconsistencies in dietary preferences defies explanation. Perhaps it is this very uncertainty that adds to the charm of bass fishing. You never are sure just what to expect of them.

For instance—by and large, a fat helgramite is relished by almost any bass, large or small. Even in lakes, where helgramites are not native and where the bass probably have never so much as seen these big larvae, they make excellent bait. Largemouth seem to like them just as well as the Smallmouth do. Naturally, you would suppose that a "hatch" of helgramites, winging its erratic way over the surface of a bass stream in annual nuptial flight, would present an enticing meal to the bass in that stream. Yet I have stood in the Delaware many times, clawing flying helgramites off the back of my neck, and watched dozens of these big insects drift fluttering down through the pool without exciting any undue interest on the part of the bass. Now and then a fish will rise and take one of them but repeated experiment has shown that these, more often than not, are big river chub and not bass. It may be that in the dormant process preparatory to sprouting wings, when the helgramite larvae leave the stream and spend a week or so hidden under rocks or logs on the bank, they undergo a change that renders them less tasty. About that I can only guess. The fact remains that the bass don't seem to care for them particularly, whereas before they change to winged insects—while they are in the true larval state— bass go for them in a big way.

In waters where crawfish are plentiful, we know that bass feed upon them regularly. They form a stable article of daily diet, and they make wonderful bass food. In the North Branch of the Susquehanna the waters abound with crawfish. Rarely do you dress a bass taken from that river that does not have a crawfish claw or two in its stomach. Yet any of the natives of that section will tell you that crawfish—craw-

The old covered bridge at Deposit, New York.

Shore-line fishing with a bass bug in the upper Delaware.

Food and Feeding Habits of Bass

dads—make one of the least productive baits that a man can use in that river.

And here is another inconsistency—from the first of July until the frosts of late September, the little stone catfish, which makes its home under the stones of the backwaters and the tributaries of the North Branch, heads the list of productive baits. A North Branch fisherman uses minnows and "shiners" —"minnies" they call them; we don't have "minnows" in central Pennsylvania—only when he can find no stone catfish or helgramites. With the coming of fall, however, the choice is reversed. Then minnows are taken avidly and stone catfish are practically ignored. Why this should be so, I'm not prepared to say, but that does not alter the fact that it is true.

And here's another unexplainable—in a Largemouth lake or pond, where minnows, shiners, insect larvae, and such are the order of the day, one of the best baits is the "night walker" or "dew worm," which is another way of saying "large angle worm." Even in a spring-fed pond, where there is little likelihood of any earthworms ever being washed in by heavy rains, the fact remains that night walkers, the bigger the better, make excellent bait.

Bass take surprisingly large creatures when the occasion presents itself. With my own two eyes, I saw a big Smallmouth in the upper Delaware roll up and take a swimming mole one day. The mole, for reasons best known to moles, had decided to cross the river, and he had the bad judgment to do so in a deep pool. Had he chosen shallower water, probably he would have been safe enough. As it was, he made an excellent meal for that big bass. There was no smashing strike or undue commotion. The bass merely drifted up to the surface, opened his mouth, and disappeared again. The mole was gone and that was that.

A friend of mine told me of seeing the same thing happen to a red squirrel in a Largemouth lake one day. This time

Black Bass

the strike was different—a typical Largemouth smash, which sent water flying in all directions.

The upper end of the two-mile-long Terrytown "level" in the North Branch of the Susquehanna is a famous place for big Smallmouth. The river bends here and the current flows fresh and strong against a masonwork wall that has been installed by the railroad company to ensure the safety of its tracks. We were fishing along this wall one day. There was a scattering of Mayflies on the water and now and then a fish would rise and take one of them.

As luck would have it, I glanced upstream just as a little songbird fluttered down from one of the trees and flew out over the water to pick up a Mayfly. Evidently he was new at that sort of thing as he made two or three passes before he managed to pick up his Mayfly. When the little bird was about a foot above the water, a big Smallmouth darted out from the shore and leaped into the air, missing the tiny bird by inches. The little fellow was so frightened that he dropped his Mayfly as he fled toward the friendly shelter of the trees.

Years ago, anglers learned that goldfish made good bass bait. These little fish, as you know, will live almost indefinitely in warm, stagnant water and this faculty makes them easy to transport without loss. The boys would buy them in the five-and-ten for a nickel or a dime apiece, and they caught fish to beat the band. I know of one hatchery that keeps a static supply of goldfish swimming about in one of the holding ponds where the bass can feed on them when they feel like it.

Just a word of caution here—don't let a warden catch you with a bucket of goldfish on any bass waters. Most states have passed strict laws against the use of goldfish as bait and the fine is apt to be pretty steep. The reason behind the formation of these anti-goldfish laws is a good one. Many fishermen were careless and small goldfish were released in bass waters where they managed to survive. Once established, they mul-

Food and Feeding Habits of Bass

tiplied so fast that they took over the water, consuming all of the food and crowding out the other fish. Goldfish can ruin a good bass pond in a surprisingly short time.

The sort of food that a bass eats seems to have a decided effect on his quality as table fare. Bass in the upper Deleware live, mostly, on insect larvae and short-line minnows. There are few crawfish in the Delaware, so that delicacy is denied the Delaware bass. In the North Branch there is a bountiful supply of crawfish and the bass feast upon them steadily. The result is that North Branch bass are so far superior in flavor to Delaware bass that there is really no comparison. They taste like two different species of fish, yet they are both river Smallmouth. The bass of the upper Mississippi River live, to a great extent, on crawfish. The banks of the sloughs (pronounced "slews") and backwaters around Prairie du Chien are fairly lined with crawfish houses, and the bass that are taken from those waters certainly are tasty items on the table.

The growth of a bass depends, to a great extent, upon how much food he consumes. Of course, water temperatures have their effect on growth, too, and a bass in cold water usually does not grow as fast as a bass that lives in moderate temperatures, but, by and large, food consumption and growth are in direct ratio. As I understand it, a bass must eat about ten pounds of food to put on a pound in weight. He doesn't begin to need all of the food he usually puts away. A pound of his natural food, spaced into regular intervals, will keep a pound of fish alive and reasonably healthy for about a year, but, if he wants to put on weight, he must feed almost constantly, as it takes a pretty liberal helping of insects, minnows, and so on to add up to a pound in weight.

Young bass are insatiable feeders. They grow to around two inches in a short time, usually in the space of several weeks from the time they leave the nest. In the upper Delaware, baby bass generally reach an average of two inches around August first, and these little fish hatch from the eggs

45

Black Bass

sometimes between May fifteenth and June fifteenth unless weather and water conditions are very much against them. By the time fall arrives, they are about four or five inches long, and by the middle of the following season a great many of them are of "legal size." Some of them, the more active feeders, reach a length of a foot or more, and weigh from three quarters of a pound to a pound during their second year.

From then until they reach maturity, they will add about a pound a year—sometimes a little less—so that by the time they become adult bass at the end of three or four years they weigh from three to four pounds. From that point on, growth depends entirely upon disposition. Some bass, like some people, are steady feeders, and these are the fish that are recorded on the *Field and Stream* record sheets. Others eat only enough to satisfy their appetites and keep them in good condition; consequently, their growth is slow as the seasons pass.

Of course, to grow big bass the water in which they live must contain a bountiful supply of natural food. If a bass can pick up a full meal for himself without too much effort, it logically follows that he will probably eat more than he will if he really has to go out and hustle to find a meal. But the story does not end there. For some reason, there is quite a definite ratio between the depth of a body of water and the average size of the bass it contains. Why this should be so I'm not prepared to say, but the fact remains that deep waters produce big fish and shallow waters produce smaller fish. This rule would seem to be contradicted by the fact that one of the world's record Smallmouths was caught in Lake Apopka, Florida. This fourteen pounder, which was taken by Walter Harden in 1932, came from a lake that averages about six feet in depth—definitely a shallow-water lake. But I happen to know that the fish came from the Oakland end of the lake where the water is spring fed, cool, and around forty or fifty feet deep. This fish has since been removed to

Food and Feeding Habits of Bass

second place by a fourteen and a half pounder, from Lake Tsala, Apopka, Florida, caught by Kenneth Curtis in 1941.

The world's record Largemouth was taken in 1932 in Montgomery Lake, Georgia, by George W. Perry. Perhaps that statement should be amended somewhat. That is the world's record bass of which an official record has been made. Dr. Henshall lists a bass that was caught in a "clear, deep, lily-bound lake" near Altoona, Florida, that weighed twenty-three and one eighth pounds, this one taken by H. W. Ross. My old St. Johns River guide, Bob Wall, told me that he had weighed bass at his fishing camp that topped the twenty-six-pound mark—not one, but several—but that these fish had never been recorded.

You have no doubt noted that all of these monsters are Southern bass. Fish don't grow that big in the North. The frigid temperatures of Northern bass waters slow down the physical activities of a bass—digestion, heartbeat, metabolism, and so on—so that the fish either go into hibernation or become dormant for about three months of the year, feeding little or not at all. Lacking tissue-building fuel, bass don't grow during these periods of hibernation and inactivity.

In the South, however, higher temperatures allow the bass to feed during the full twelve months of the year, with the result that they grow to greater size. In Florida, yearling bass—fish that are about midway in their second year—are apt to weigh from one and a half to two and a half pounds. In the North, a six-pound Smallmouth or an eight-pound Largemouth probably will walk off with a good share of the big-fish prizes for the year. In the South, bass of these weights, while they are unquestionably "nice fish," excite only passing interest.

Every now and then, a bass lake or pond will go out of balance so that the food supply is entirely inadequate to meet the demand. When this happens, the bass must get along on a

Black Bass

starvation diet, and their general bodily condition shows it. I have had the dubious privilege of fishing two such lakes.

The first one I encountered is a private pond owned by a rather exclusive sportsmen's club on Long Island. The members felt that they weren't taking their full quotas of bass from that pond so they decided to give Nature a hand and do some stocking. I fished it about two years after this stocking had been done. Believe me, they must have poured in truckload after truckload of young bass, as the pond was alive with stunted bass that ran in size from ten to twelve inches. These little fish welcomed anything that so much as suggested food, and catching them soon grew tiresome. All of them had large heads and pitifully small, emaciated, underdeveloped bodies. None of them weighed more than half what they should have weighed. In short, they couldn't find enough food to make a decent living. But here's a strange commentary on that pond. Here and there leftovers from the prestocking days, old, adult bass, would come to your lure if you fished diligently and carefully. There was no difficulty in finding these big fish. If you cast several times about a "bassy" looking area without hooking any of the little underfed bass, you knew that you were casting within the territorial boundaries of one of the big fish. Evidently they would drive all other fish away from their chosen feeding areas.

I had been told about these old busters before we went out on the pond and, largely through great good fortune, I managed to hook one of them. He lived under a stump, the top of which was barely submerged, so I cast a bass bug over the top of the stump, hoping that the stump itself would keep him from seeing me. Sure enough, up he came and took the bug into camp with a smashing strike that could be heard all over the pond. He weighed about six pounds and gave me quite an argument. All of that was in order and to be expected. What I did not expect was to find him in such excellent physical condition. I don't think I have ever seen a fatter,

Food and Feeding Habits of Bass

huskier potbellied Largemouth. In a lake that was almost denuded of food, this old citizen managed to find enough to keep him fat, sassy, and beautifully conditioned. His stomach was empty so there was no telling what he used for food, but I wouldn't be greatly surprised if his diet consisted mostly of his lesser relatives.

At the time I fished that pond, the club was attempting to undo the damage they had done. They were seining out small bass by the tubful and transferring them to other waters. Then they planned to stock with minnows and golden shiners. Eventually, I suppose, they can bring the pond back to normal, but it's going to be quite a job.

The other pond that was out of balance is in the rolling sand hills of northern Wisconsin. At the invitation of the Wisconsin Conservation Commission, Dick and I had gone out there to look over the bass fishing. After spending a delightful week in the Mississippi sloughs around Prairie du Chien, we drove north to do some fishing for Smallmouth and Musky. The weather had been threatening for several days, and on the way we encountered rain. And I mean *rain*. Several times we had to stop the car, turn on the lights, so we wouldn't be hit by other cars, and wait until we could see the road ahead of us.

Eventually we arrived at Ed Nutt's camp on the banks of the Namakagon River. It was after dark when we drove in, and still raining. Mrs. Nutt gave us a snack, and we turned in early.

All night the rain pounded on the roof, but about dawn the downpour stopped and morning dawned bright and clear. You can imagine our dismay when we opened the door of our cabin to find the river we intended to fish about eight feet over its banks and already covering at least half of the sloping lawn. The dock was four or five feet under water. Dick and some of the guides spent part of the morning retrieving boat trailers and boats from the flood.

Black Bass

River fishing being out of the question for at least two weeks, he had to fall back on lake fishing. Fearing that this might be the case, the evening before we had engaged a filling-station attendant in conversation about the bass fishing. After we had filled the car with gas, bought some oil, and then purchased a knife and some bass plugs at his tackle counter, he waxed confidential. There was a lake, he told us, not far from Ed's camp, called Bass Lake. From its crystal waters had been extracted, no less than the week before, a twelve-pound Largemouth. The lake wasn't on the map, but maybe we could find a guide who knew where it lay.

We made due allowance for enthusiasm and hearsay, but the lake still sounded pretty good. As I had suspected, Ed, who is a forest ranger, knew exactly where it was, so we drove over—cross-country, there being no road—to look it over, dragging two boats on a trailer behind the car.

Bass Lake proved to be a crescent-shaped affair that nestled in a fold in the hills. It was about half a mile long and perhaps two hundred yards wide at its widest part. The water was gin-clear and its shores were lined with excellent cover—treetops, logs, reeds, rushes, lily pads, and so on. It looked mighty interesting.

Bass Lake proved to be another Stump Pond, Long Island. There were little underfed bass by the thousand, all anxious to fall upon a bass bug and tear it to ribbons. They had the typical oversize heads and shrunken bodies and it was quite obvious that their growth had been badly stunted.

Here and there, however, I managed to raise an old buster of a bass. These whoppers, unfortunately, showed a tendency to come short. They weren't feeding, merely curious, and they would come up to look the bug over. This done, they would retire to their hidyholes with a swirl and a splash that made my sparse locks stand on end. Only one of them actually took the bug and this was one of the lesser ones, a midget of three and a half pounds. Unlike his smaller brothers and sisters

Food and Feeding Habits of Bass

with the big heads and small bodies, this fellow was well conditioned and fat, and he showed every indication of being able to find all the food he wanted. I suspected cannibalism although, as before, there was no incriminating evidence in his stomach.

Even in lakes where there is plenty of food, once in a while you will find a bass that shows unmistakable signs of malnutrition. Derby Pond, near Newport, Vermont, holds food aplenty and its Largemouth are deep, heavy fish. George Donovan and I were fishing Derby Pond one day, he rowing while I cast a plug along the deep shore line. The plug I had chosen was a buxom affair, in reality a Musky plug. It was composed of three sections, jointed together with flexible links; it was pink (that's right, so help me) scale finish, and it weighed seven-eighths of an ounce. Its general appearance and the seductive motion with which it moved through the water had prompted Dick and me to christen it Mae West.

I had cast Mae beside a bush that hung out over the point of land at one corner of a rather large cove. After a few preliminary wiggles, I started Mae on her wobbling trip back to the boat. She hadn't gone four feet before there was a tremendous splash and flurry of water, and I found myself fast to a bass.

George shot the boat toward deep water and the bass and I decided matters forthwith. I thought at the time that the fight was in no way commensurate with the strike and when the bass was in the boat we found out why. Consider these specifications—the bass measured a little over two feet long; from point of lower jaw, mouth closed, to the rear of the gill cover was six and a quarter inches; *and,* the bass weighed exactly one and three-quarter pounds. Why, in a lake where there was plenty of food, a bass should place itself on a self-imposed starvation diet I can't imagine. Its body was the size and general conformation of a grass pickerel. The fish seemed to be perfectly healthy when George and I performed an autopsy. Evidently, there was little food available near its chosen living quarters and it was just too darned lazy to go out and rustle up a meal every day. In good condition that Largemouth should have weighed six or seven pounds.

As I say, bass are peculiar creatures, cranky, cantankerous, unpredictable, and often completely exasperating. Rarely, if ever, do I venture forth on lake or stream that I don't learn something about them. But that's the way I like them. If they always conformed to a set pattern of behavior, a great deal of the charm of fishing for them would be lost. However, I guess I needn't worry about that. There is little likelihood that they will change.

CHAPTER 4

Bass Rods

UNLIKE MOST SORTS OF fresh-water fishing, bass fishing requires rods of two distinct models—three, really, now that
thread-line fishing, "spinning," "slip casting," or what have
you, has come into vogue. To fish for bass properly, with
artificial lures, a man must have at least one fly rod and one
casting rod. Otherwise, he will find himself greatly handi-
capped now and then. Perhaps the spinning rod could be considered as excess cargo when you want to strip down to bare
necessities, but you definitely should have the other two. Most
ardent bass anglers have a great many more rods than that
and all of these have their uses once in a while.

It is a common fallacy among anglers that they tend to
skimp on their bass equipment. A trout fisherman will spend
days, weeks, and sometimes years, trying to find the perfect
fly rod. But he is content to use most any old thing for his
bass fishing, providing that it has some backbone and will
stand heavy going. Possibly this accounts for the lamentable
truth that there are exceedingly few finished bass fishermen.
I know literally thousands of fishermen, yet in all this multitude I can number only four men who can handle a bass fly
rod the way it should be handled—five, if we include my son
Dick.

Black Bass

Regardless of this, few companies put out good bass fly rods. Moreover, they don't take the trouble to find out exactly what action is necessary in order to have a fly rod qualify as a really good tool for bass fishing. Sure, I know, there are a lot of "bass-bug rods" on the market, but 99 per cent of them are stiff, clubby, top-action mongrels that are not worth the room they take up. No use kidding yourself—a good workman, or a good fisherman, can't turn out a top-notch job with poor tools.

One summer recently we held, as usual, our annual sportsmen's field day here in Lycoming County, Pennsylvania. There was trapshooting, skeet shooting, target shooting with rifle and pistol, bait casting, and fly casting, not to mention many minor events and exhibitions to keep the customers happy. I dropped in at the fishing events. There, standing in a rack, were several fly rods, equipped with reels, lines, leaders, and tournament flies. These rods were there to be used by anybody who hadn't taken the trouble to bring his own tackle. Being "loan" rods, I didn't expect too much, but I was amazed to learn what can be done in the way of poor rod construction. It has always been my opinion that, merely because a rod is turned out to sell for ten or fifteen dollars, it does not necessarily follow that it must be badly designed. Even though second-grade or third-grade wood is used in its construction, a cheap rod can be designed so that it has a reasonably usable action.

The rods that were standing there in the rack for general use were, I observed, all made by the same company. There being both distance and accuracy events scheduled, the rods chosen were big ones, nine-foot-six in length. There wasn't one of the four that weighed less than seven and a half ounces. Curious to see what they would do, I picked one up and went over to the practice range. Try as I would, I couldn't get out more than sixty-five feet of line. The rod was a top-action affair and as soon as any line load to speak of was brought to

Bass Rods

bear, the tip and upper middle joint would bog down and the lower rod would come through with all the svelte, flexible grace of a broomstick. Then I went back to the rack and looked at the other three rods. Evidently a mistake had been made at the factory as one of them was a little better than the others. Or maybe that one had been made of softer wood —anyway, there was some slight sign of usable action in the lower rod. With a great deal of effort, perfect timing, and the help of a light following wind, I actually did manage a cast of seventy-eight feet. Incidentally, that was the record cast for those four rods for the two days of the field-day contests.

Now, I'm no distance caster—just an ordinary bass fisherman who likes fine tackle. But with my own bass-bug rod, which has been carefully designed for the job and is made of the finest wood available, I can do seventy-eight feet with my left hand, blindfolded.

The sequel to the above recitation came the following week. I happened to drop into the sporting-goods store which had supplied these four wonder-rods for the field-day contests. There they were, standing in the display rack, being offered at reduced prices. And they were labeled "Bass-bug Rods."

Some years before there were such things as bass bugs for sale in the sporting-goods stores—way back around 1915, to be exact—I started fooling around with bass fly rods. It didn't take me long to find out that a cheap rod, bought for this purpose, was merely a waste of money. In the first place, bass are rugged citizens. They are masters in the art of surprise and they are apt to strike when you least expect it. After smashing several cheap rods beyond all hope of repair, I began to look around for a *good* bass fly rod. After considerable search, I came to the conclusion that the local stores had no such thing in stock. Accordingly, I decided to make one.

At one of our stores there was an elderly man who repaired guns and tackle, and he had some glued-up sticks and fittings in stock. I explained to him what I had in mind and together we went through his pile of rod sections until we found about what we wanted. Purposely, we picked out four sections that were slightly oversize. Then came ferrules, reel seat, guides, etc. I asked questions and listened to instructions until I felt that I knew what to do. Then I gathered up my mess of rod materials, took them home, and went to work. Lacking cork rings for the grip, I substituted thermos-bottle corks and they worked all right.

When the oversize sections were set up and assembled I had a rod that was ten-feet-six long, limber and loose as a buggy whip. Then, gradually, I worked the rod down for size and action. Cut and try, cut and try; half an inch here, an eighth there, until I was completely sick of the whole blooming business. At long last, I had the rod in what I hoped would be final form. It was nine-feet-nine long and weighed six and a half ounces.

The following season, on "opening day," I took it with me to the Delaware and gave it its first trial run. My, what a relief to have a bass fly rod that would do what I wanted a rod to do. That one day's fishing made the trials and tribulations of the winter before seem worth while. The action was slow but powerful and, compared to the performances of previous rods, it seemed to throw a bass streamer a country mile.

I still have that old rod, and now and then, just for old time's sake, I take it out and use it. Battered and beaten as it is, it still stands up and continues to cast well, although I must confess that I am more gentle with it than I am with rods of more recent manufacture. With it I have caught thousands of bass. I have used it for salmon, taking fish up to eighteen pounds with it. And when the time came for me to design a bass-bug rod for one of the factories, that was one of the models that contributed greatly to the formation of the taper of the Knight Ninety-Nine bass-bug rod that is now sold commercially.

Bass Rods

There is quite a little diversity of opinion among the men who write books and articles about bass fishing, concerning the importance of the bass fly rod and also its correct use. We will go into angling methods later on. It should be said here, however, that a good bass fly rod is one designed to enable the angler to handle from sixty to eighty or ninety feet of line. Not only that, but the rod should do this chore without placing undue strain on the angler's casting hand, so that he can fish with that rod for several hours at a time without putting his arm out of business. A tournament rod, with power to spare, will lay out that much line without any trouble, but it is apt to wreck your casting hand in half an hour or so. Such a rod is designed for greater distances and therefore has excess power which can, if desired, be put to work. A bass fly rod, if it is made properly, will perform most efficiently at distances that range from sixty to eighty feet. These ranges can be reached almost without effort if the rod is used correctly. On the other hand, the rod begins to lose efficiency at eighty-five or ninety feet. It just isn't meant to handle that much line. In other words, it is a bass fly rod, not a tournament distance rod.

Few casting-rod fans can see any merit in the fly rod and they don't hesitate to say so. One man I know—and, believe me, he's a sound bass fisherman—calls bass-bug fishing "skittering." Another goes into some detail to explain how ridiculously simple it is to learn to use a fly rod. Nothing to it. Then he goes on to say that his preference for the casting rod is based on the fact that he likes to fish at least sixty-five or seventy feet from the boat and the fly rod is not practical at that range. It looks as though it's about time we boys got together and straightened out a few of these kinks.

This is the way I see it. I like a casting rod for some purposes. It will handle lures that a fly rod can not handle—obviously it is impractical to attempt to cast a bass plug with a fly rod—and it will enable you to fish underwater lures at depths that are entirely impractical for a fly rod. There are a great many things that an angler can do with a casting rod that he can't begin to duplicate with a fly rod. Rarely, if ever, do I go on a fishing trip without taking a couple of casting outfits with me.

By the same token, a fly rod will do quite a number of things that can't possibly be done with a casting rod. First off, it will handle small lures at reasonably long distances. With a casting rod you would have trouble throwing these same lures more than ten feet—hair frogs, for instance, or Fred Geist's Powder Puff, or Joe Messinger's deer-hair Nite Hummer, all exceedingly effective lures. A good bass fly rod will handle these small-size lures lightly and accurately at the distances they should be fished—from sixty to eighty feet. For fishing the duckwort beds in the sloughs and backwaters of the upper Mississippi, there can be no possible argument in favor of any lure but the bass bug. And you can't handle a bass bug with a casting rod. For handling weedless lures in the back-behind spots of a big-mouth lake—places where few men fish and where the big bass live—a weedless fly-rod lure is more practical because it is light. And you can't cast around corners with a plug rod. With a fly rod, you can. Where the cover is thick, you can curve-cast a bug around behind stumps and into pockets that couldn't be reached otherwise. As I say, each rod has its uses and I see no point in condemning either in favor of the other.

But what qualities go to make a bass fly rod a *good* bass fly rod? First off, a bass fly rod should not be less than nine-foot-six. Sure, I know—a nine-foot, five-and-three-quarter-ounce, tournament-action rod will heave out a bass bug for you as far as you want it to go. But for how long? My casting hand won't stand up with one of those power plants for more than half an hour. The nine-foot-six, nine-foot-nine, or ten-foot bass fly rod gives you a higher lift in your back cast with less effort, and the extra length permits the maker to

John Woodhull's line basket is very handy for the long caster. Slack line can be coiled in the basket, thus facilitating the shoot.

Fishing the duckwort beds of the "slews" near Prairie du Chien, Wisconsin. Here a weedless bug is essential.

Typical Largemouth from the Mississippi duckwort beds.

Bass Rods

slow down the action to the point where it fits bass-bug timing. So much for the length.

Your fly rod should weigh from six and a quarter to six and three quarters ounces, a good deal of this weight difference being taken up by the sort of fittings used. This much weight will let the maker put in a little extra wood so that you have a certain reserve of power that is not ordinarily used. As I say, the action of the rod should be slow, and it should be distributed throughout the entire rod, right down to the grip. My personal preference does not lean toward the uniform taper. I think you get better performance and more power with less effort if the middle rod is stiffened slightly—and I mean only slightly; otherwise the rod speeds up and makes timing difficult—so that there is an indication of "semiparabolic" lever action in the part of the rod that is made up of the upper third of the butt joint and the lower two thirds of the middle joint. This sort of fly rod makes bass-bug casting a joy. All you need to do is pick up the line and lure from the water and wait for the rod to throw the back cast up and out behind you. Then you give the handle a push, followed by an effortless "throwing-in" of the rod tip at the finish, and the rod goes to work for you while you hang on and watch your forward cast roll out and complete itself. With this sort of rod, long-line casting can be effortless and pleasant— and very efficient and effective.

When you expect a fly rod to do long-line casting for you with comparatively heavy lures, such as bass bugs, you should make up your mind that you must pay for top-quality materials. Second-grade wood simply will not stand up under such heavy work, and you are wasting money to buy anything but the best. Oh, once in a while you might be lucky enough to find a cheap fly rod that will stand up under bass-bug casting, but the probabilities are that it won't. If you finish one season with a cheap rod remaining intact, you have

Black Bass

been lucky. Better spend sixty dollars or so and get a good one.

Rod fittings are important, too. I don't mind adding a little weight to a rod if I'm sure that it will have plenty of backbone. Don't make the mistake of buying a rod that is equipped with spun ferrules. These are easy to distinguish as they have rolled welts at the tops of the female ferrules. Usually they are made of brass tubing, spun into shape and nickel plated. They cost about twenty cents a set and are not worth that much so far as durability is concerned. Make sure that your ferrules are drawn from German silver stock, hand-welted, lathe-turned, waterproofed (meaning a metal partition down

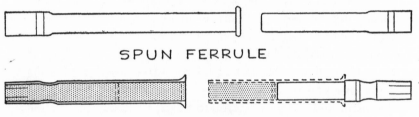

SPUN FERRULE

HIGH-GRADE FERRULE
(CROSS SECTION)

inside the female ferrule), and serrated to a knife edge where metal meets wood, this to help to absorb sudden shocks. On good rods you will find top-grade ferrules anyway, but watch for spun ferrules on medium-priced rods. If you buy them, you are due for ferrule trouble all too soon. Agate tip guides and an agate hand guide or "stripping guide" will allow a better shoot for your line, but tungsten or Mildarbide will last longer because they won't crack as readily if you happen to tap them against a rock. The snake guides should definitely be oversize. A nylon bass fly line has a rather large diameter and trout-size guides set up too much guide friction, cutting down your shoot on the forward cast. It is not desirable to have too many guides on a bass fly rod. Again, if

Bass Rods

you have too few, the line will sag slightly, thus increasing line friction. On a bass fly rod, I prefer two guides on the butt joint, four on the middle joint, and five on the tips, not including the tip guides.

Brown-tone wood is all right for a heavy-duty rod of this sort, always providing that the heat treatment, which gives the wood its brown color, is done properly in an oven and not with a blow torch. By and large, well-seasoned tonkin cane in its natural yellow tone is about as good as you can find in rod wood. It is tough and resilient and it holds its life exceedingly well. With reasonable care, a good rod of yellow tonkin cane will last you a lifetime. Above all things, don't buy a rod of "flamed" wood—one having a mottling of brown spots on the natural yellow. While a rod thus treated may be a bit livelier at first, the flaming process sets up internal stresses in the rod sections that do not make for durability.

When you come right down to it, your best guarantee that a rod is all that it should be is to buy one that has been made by a manufacturer of good reputation. There are a great many things, not visible to external inspection, that can make a rod a good one or a bad one. Faulty workmanship doesn't show on the surface, so play safe and buy a rod of reliable make. You may pay more but you will get your money's worth.

Over the years a great many materials have been used in rod construction. As a matter of fact, there probably isn't a wood that grows that has not, one time or another, been used for this purpose. Some of them, notably greenheart and lancewood, made fairly satisfactory fly rods before the development of the split bamboo rod. However, the weight-to-resiliency ratio of good butt-cut tonkin cane is so much more favorable for fly-rod use that today this is the accepted material for good fly rods.

Some of the companies have done wonders with steel. The

fly rods that they turn out with this material are creditable pieces of workmanship, but they are fighting an uphill battle, as the inherent characteristics of steel do not lend themselves to fly-rod construction so readily as tonkin cane does. I have several of these steel rods and they are reliable, tough pieces of equipment that will stand up under all sorts of rough handling, but all of them lack the "feel" and action of bamboo.

In the spring of 1944, three of us journeyed to North Carolina to explore the possibilities of the brackish-water fishing for Largemouth around Currituck Sound and the general vicinity of Kitty Hawk. Here the wind blows almost constantly—that is why the Wright brothers chose these shifting sand dunes for their early experiments in aviation. We fished bass bug almost exclusively and, as you know, a bass bug is generally more effective when fished in quiet water. Thus we found it to our advantage to fish the calm shore line under the lee of the high reeds of the marsh. This meant casting directly into the wind and, in consequence, applying to each cast from twice to three times the power that ordinarily would have been necessary. It was a punishing task for a fly rod. After an hour or so with my pet bamboo rod, punching each cast into the wind and up under the lee of the marsh, I decided that it was not wise to subject the rod to such continued strain. Accordingly, I put away my tonkin-cane rod and set up a steel fly rod. For six full days I drove that heavy line and bass bug up into a fairly strong wind, making no effort to spare the steel rod in any way, and putting all the force and power into each cast that was needed to place the bass bug where I wanted it to go. A tougher assignment couldn't be set up to test the staying powers of any fly rod, but that nine-foot, five-and-three-quarter-ounce steel rod finished up the trip as straight and true as when it started.

My friends were using bamboo rods. One of these stood the test in good shape and, for that matter, is still going strong

Bass Rods

under continued hard usage. The other rod, a fairly new one, developed a fault in the upper middle joint and, almost without warning, came unglued, all six strips parting company like the ribs of an umbrella in a strong wind. However, it was the gluing, after all, and not the wood, that let go.

There are two plastic processes currently on the market that will no doubt have a marked effect on rods and rod materials. The first is the Bakelite impregnation process whereby first-grade tonkin cane is thoroughly saturated with Bakelite. This Bakelite solution, when hardened, serves a triple purpose. It seems to add life and resiliency to the cane, it serves as a binder that glues the strips of the rod sections together, and it waterproofs the rod sections completely, eliminating the need of protective coats of varnish.

While he had no active part in the actual work of impregnating the first rod with Bakelite, I feel that the original idea should be credited to that versatile angler, Edward Ringwood Hewitt. I happened to be at his camp on the Neversink one week end while Mr. and Mrs. George W. Bakeland were there as guests. Mr. Bakeland's father was the inventor of the plastic, Bakelite. Mr. Hewitt explained his idea, showing how the impregnation of bamboo could be accomplished, and outlining the probable beneficial results. Some two years later, largely as the direct result of this conversation, a fly rod was thus built at the Perth Amboy, New Jersey, plant of the Bakelite Corporation under the direction of Mr. Rossi who was then, I believe, plant manager. As a matter of fact, I am quite sure that Mr. Rossi, himself an ardent angler, planed out the strips of bamboo that were used in that first Bakelite fly rod. In the winter of 1938-1939, he brought it with him to my class in fresh-water angling, then being held at Columbia University, and I showed the rod to that group of about eighty people, explaining its construction. These rods are now on the market and are standing the test of time very well indeed.

Black Bass

The other plastic process is known as the "glass rod." This process was developed at the plant of the Owens-Illinois Glass Company and the original manufacturing franchise was granted to the Shakespeare Company. The rod sections are molded forms, composed of spun-glass filaments held together with one of the resin plastics. As this is written, the process is too new to have proven itself, but I have seen and handled two of these rods and the material shows a great deal of promise. How it will stand up under hard usage remains to be seen.

When thinking of substitute materials for rod construction, naturally the thought comes to mind that so long as tonkin cane has all of the qualities that are needed for rod building, why worry about synthetic substitutes? In reply, there is every reason to seek such materials. Tonkin cane must be imported and we in the United States have no control over the supply of raw cane. No two pieces of tonkin cane are exactly alike, with the result that two fly rods, cut to identical specifications and tapers, differ somewhat in action. It is exceedingly difficult to duplicate exactly a fly rod of tonkin cane. With a substitute of known characteristics, which can be standardized and manufactured in bulk, this variation in the quality of materials no longer exists. A tonkin-cane rod, a good one, is an expensive thing to manufacture. A great deal of highly skilled handwork is required in its construction.

With a material of standardized characteristics and unlimited supply, mass-production methods are both possible and practical, and rods of proven design and performance can be turned out in quantity and with much less expense. In short, with a *good* substitute material—and by that, I mean as good as or better than tonkin cane—a man can buy a rod of standard specifications that will turn out a satisfactory casting job for him, thus eliminating the present gamble as to lasting quality and action that is inherent in the purchase of a tonkin-cane rod. To be sure, substitute materials will remove some of the "romance of angling," but they will place good, usable rods within reach of the average pocketbook and give a man his money's worth when he buys a rod.

The selection of a casting rod should be attended by just as much thought and care as the purchase of a fly rod. Just as there is no all-purpose fly rod, there is also no casting rod that will give you good performance on all types of bait casting. Obviously, the rod that will handle, neatly and accurately, a quarter-ounce or a three-eighth-ounce lure will be of little use with a three-quarter-ounce musky plug. Thus, an angler should have not less than two casting outfits—one to handle the light lures and one for the heavier baits.

While I do not believe that steel can ever be in the same class with bamboo as a rod material, there is no doubt that steel casting rods are good, sturdy tools, particularly for handling the heavier lures. For the lighter, finer outfits, however, bamboo is in a class by itself.

In the matter of length, I believe that that is largely one of preference. Unquestionably, the longer, more flexible rods are better for light-lure casting. For half-ounce and five-eighth-ounce lures, however, my leaning is toward the five-and-a-half-foot rod of medium action, fairly well distributed throughout the whole rod.

When speaking of action in a casting rod, I am assuming, naturally, that you are an overhead caster. That is the only sort of bait-casting that places any emphasis on action in a casting rod. If you happen to be a side-swing caster—which I hope you are not—don't bother to read this. Any old rod will sideswipe a bait out for you. For that matter, a broomstick will serve all right for a side-wheeler. His method employs the use of rod, reel, hand, wrist, forearm, elbow, shoulder, and, sometimes, torso and legs. Rod action is lost in the shuffle—as are, all too frequently, sundry portions of the anatomies of his boat companions. I'd far rather gun with a man who hunts with his safety off than ride in the same boat with a side-wheel caster. I'd be safer. The last time I had that dubious pleasure, my companion broke a cedar plug against the side of my head. That's right. We were fishing for big sea trout around the pilings of an old wharf in Pensacola Bay and my companion caught me, full swing, just above my left ear with a three-quarter-ounce cedar plug. Fortunately I was wearing a felt hat with the brim turned up. When I came to, half of that plug was fastened to his line and the other half hung from the brim of my hat. Right then I vowed to steer clear of side-wheel casters.

With the shorter, more powerful five-foot or five-and-a-half-foot rod that you need for five-eighth-ounce lures, the casting motion is somewhat faster and requires more effort. But if you have to make work out of it, your' rod is too stiff for the job. Remember that action is built into a casting rod for the convenience and comfort of the angler. If this same action, with only the absolute minimum of effort on your part, isn't putting your plug out there where you want it, then your outfit probably isn't balanced properly, and you'd better have it looked over by a man who knows casting outfits.

Back in 1925, when we lived in Florida, I used to fish with a "Florida rod." This was a four-and-a-half-foot affair, bamboo, with a solid, stocky butt and a fairly light tip. We fished five-eighth- and three-quarter-ounce plugs, mostly, and a good share of our fishing was "pocket fishing"—spotting the plug into holes in the lily pads or water hyacinths, behind logs and into the difficult out-of-the-way-places. If no strike greeted the plug, then, in order to retrieve it without being "hung up," we used to "jump it out"—jerk it free of the water so that it would sail back to our general vicinity by the aerial route. This eliminated annoying complications with snags and vegetation and was a definite timesaver. For that

Bass Rods

sort of fishing you need a stiff, strong rod. I still have that old rod, and just to pick it up today makes my casting arm tired. But I've taken bass with it, hundreds and hundreds of bass, ranging up to fourteen pounds. I don't use it any more, but I like to have it around as a memento of the truly superlative bass fishing that we used to find in obscure Florida lakes and the headwaters of the St. Johns River.

As you know, no two casting outfits handle exactly alike. Thus, no two casters employ identical casting motions or favor the same outfits. Unlike fly-rod fishing, bait casting allows an angler a great deal more latitude in the selection of his tackle. For that reason, when discussing casting rods, it is possible to deal only with generalities, based on a few solid fundamentals.

It is best to have a locking reel seat—most of them are, anyway, these days, and the old slip ring that would work loose and let your reel tumble off is pretty much a thing of the past. It is better to get a reel seat that has its fixed socket toward the tip end of your rod. This is the socket that takes all the strain, and the lock merely holds the reel in place. You may or may not like the offset reel seat. Either the old-style reel seat or the offset types are satisfactory. In case you haven't tried these latter, you will find that you get used to them very quickly.

Some anglers like a cigar-shaped grip on a casting rod, but my preference is a "shaped grip" with a bulge at the butt to keep it from slipping through my hand. Of course, if your rod has a trigger for your index finger there is little chance of your throwing your outfit over the side of the boat. And for my part, I like a trigger. It means that I have one less thing to think about. I have seen men throw expensive casting outfits over the side. So far, I have been lucky, but I have helped fish out three outfits that might very well have been lost if weather and water conditions had not been ideal.

Black Bass

One thing I would caution you against—the offset grip that is out of line with the rest of the rod. Sure, they're fine in theory and maybe a fellow could get used to them in time, but I feel that a rod built in a straight line from tip to butt makes for greater accuracy.

CHAPTER 5

Bass Reels

JUST AS IMPORTANT as the action and quality of a casting rod is the choice of the reel that you use on that rod. There has been a great deal of talk of "balanced tackle" for the past several years and there seems to be no clear definition or common understanding of that word balanced. No two men agree exactly on what constitutes balance among rod, reel, and line. In a casting outfit, balance adds up about like this. Your selection of rod length, rod action, reel weight, reel starting torque, and line weight should be such that the assembly will handle, smoothly, accurately, and efficiently, the types and weights of lures that you plan to use with that outfit. That's as close as I can come to putting "balanced tackle" into words. Let's see if we can't clarify it somewhat.

For instance—the average bait-casting reel that you see on a tackle counter is designed to handle five-eighth-ounce lures. In other words, the weight of the spool, the handle, and the gears (all of which have their bearing on that vital factor "starting torque") have been determined at the factory, in advance of manufacture, so that the reel will turn out its best casting job with a five-eighth-ounce lure. Obviously, this reel belongs on a rod that is designed for the same class of lures. When using this reel, your line should be in the same class—not too heavy and not too light. Then you will have a balanced outfit, and it will handle five-eighth-ounce lures for you at ordinary fishing distances with the minimum of effort and the maximum of accuracy.

Now then—suppose you put this reel on a rod that is six feet or six-foot-six long, which has a slow, well-distributed action; in short, a rod which has been set up for the express purpose of handling light lures. If you are a good caster, probably you can toss out quarter-ounce or three-eighth-ounce lures with such a mismated rig. Depend upon it, however, that your days with light lures will be far pleasanter and more productive if you buy for that rod a lighter reel that has been designed for light-lure use.

I've taken it for granted that you know that what I've just said refers to quadruple-multiplier casting reels. That's the only reel that belongs on a good casting outfit—a reel which is so geared that the spool makes four complete revolutions for every single revolution of the handle.

"Starting torque" is a variable thing. It means, briefly, the amount of energy necessary to start the spool of a reel spinning at casting speeds, this energy to be applied, of course, to the spool while it is stationary. In other words, the force necessary to overcome the inertia of the stationary spool. On some reels, starting torque is so low that even the weight of a light swivel will set the reel in motion. On others, it is so high that, even with a five-eighth-ounce lure, your thumb can be removed from the spool completely before the lure passes your shoulder on the forward cast. As I say, it is variable and no two reels have exactly the same starting torque. So many things affect it, one way or another. The viscosity of the grease or oil on the gears; the temperature of the day on which you happen to be using the reel; the weight of the spool, the reel handle, the gears, and the reel arbor; even line friction in the guides has its influence. It is this variable that is responsible,

Bass Reels

mostly, for the fact that no two casting outfits handle in exactly the same way.

About 1938, if my memory serves me correctly, a firm in Great Britain sent me a quadruple multiplier that they were then introducing to the angling market. It was a beautifully made affair, quite expensive, and finished like a Rolls Royce. British manufacturers have not had the experience with quadruple multipliers that American manufacturers have. At the factory where this reel was made, one of the engineers had designed an antibacklash attachment intended to simplify casting by eliminating backlashes. It is an ingenious affair of sliding weights, located inside the curved "disk" of the end plates of the spool. The movements of these weights are controlled by springs. Thus, at slow speeds, the weights rest against the shaft of the spool. As the speed of the spool is increased, centrifugal force pushes the weights away from the shaft, thereby applying centrifugal braking action which slows down the rate of spin and prevents the spool from overrunning the line and causing a backlash. All very well in theory, but those little weights set up the starting torque of the reel to the point where I had great difficulty in casting with it. I gave the reel to Dick (that's my son, as you no doubt know by this time) and he learned to use it. Now, having grown accustomed to the high torque, he uses it in preference to any other reel unless he happens to be fishing with light lures.

When you are buying a reel, keep this matter of starting torque in mind. In the tackle shop you won't be able to tell very much about it, but there are a few things that will tell you at least part of the story. For instance, if the reel handle is extra heavy and the spool is solidly and sturdily built, you know that the starting torque is high. Spin the reel by flipping one of your fingers against the handle. You can gauge, rather closely sometimes, whether the starting torque is high or low, merely by the pressure the handle places against your finger. However, the only way to find out definitely whether the starting torque of a reel will lend itself to your style of casting is to take the reel out and use it. Obviously, that can't be done unless you pay for it. This hurdle can be cleared if you can find an angling friend who has a similar reel. Try out his reel. If you like it, you know that the one in the shop will be enough like it to be satisfactory.

Another thing—a great many anglers determine the quality and workmanship of a reel by spinning it to see how long it will run. If the reel spins freely and continues to spin, decelerating slowly to a stop, it is a good reel. That's the test they apply. Well, of course a reel should spin freely. Perhaps I should say that a reel should spin smoothly. But you must remember that a high starting torque will help a reel to keep spinning longer than one that has a low starting torque. Next time you spin a new reel in a tackle shop, start it spinning in the upright position and then, while it is moving rapidly, turn it on its side. Nine chances to one, it will stop almost immediately. End bearings or thrust bearings in a reel are just about as important as are the bushings. If these are not properly set, any change of position will alter slightly the relative positions of the gears, and the reel will cease to function smoothly.

While I was giving my lecture course at Columbia University, some of the tackle companies used to send in sample tackle. I tried to discourage this, explaining that the course was entirely noncommercial, but they sent the tackle in anyway. One of the items was a quadruple-multiplier reel. That reel was the spinningest reel I ever saw. Start it and it would go and go and go—providing you held it upright. Tilt it slightly and it would grind to a sudden stop as though an unseen hand had grabbed it. This masterpiece listed, I believe, at $3.98 or some such silly amount. Curious to see what went on inside its shiny exterior, I took it apart one night. Oh, brother! The gears were set so that they didn't quite mesh—

Bass Reels

they merely caressed each other in passing. The bushings were loosely fitted. End play, except in the spool, evidently wasn't considered. The parts were rough, unpolished, and entirely too heavy. Only light oil had been put on the gears and bushings, so that the reel would spin to beat the band when held upright. I relegated that one to the storage cabinet and during the war, when tackle was impossible to get, I gave it to a man who had thrown his old reel overboard while fishing the North Branch. He told me he had reached the point where *anything* would be welcome.

As I write this, there lies on the desk before me a reel that was turned out for me, as a special favor, in the experimental shop of one of the big factories. At the time I was anxious to have a reel with an extremely low starting torque, so they built this one for me. The gears are exactly cut and polished. The spool is of aluminum with paper-thin plates and a hollow shaft, and the handle is built in proportion. Only with effort can this reel be spun so that the handle will make more than three full turns. Yet in actual use it is the fastest thing I have ever had on a rod.

Don't buy a reel that has too many foolproof gadgets on it. Antibacklash devices are all right, I suppose, but the best antibacklash device that has been invented to date is a well-trained thumb. Level-wind attachments do not, according to my ideas, come under the heading "gadgets." While a free-spool unadorned reel is a joy to use, it simply is not practical for shore-line fishing with a top-water bait. As a matter of fact, you will have trouble finding the old-style reels nowadays. Level-winders are so completely practical that they have just about replaced the older types. Of course, level-wind attachments do add friction and cut down casting distance, but at normal fishing ranges they function satisfactorily and they are a convenience.

Most reels are built without arbors—perhaps I should say "built-up arbors." The shaft or spindle of the spool is, in a sense, an arbor. If you plan to cast the heavier lures—half-ounce, five-eighths, or three-quarters—you can fill the spool to capacity with medium-weight line. With the light lures, however, a cork or a balsa-wood arbor is desirable. If you are mechanically minded, you can build your own arbors and fit them to your reels. If not, the repair man at the local tackle shop can do it for you. Have your arbor large enough so that it and one hundred yards of light line will fill completely the spool of your reel. If you use extra line to fill up the spool of your reel instead of using an arbor, this line gradually absorbs water and this adds weight so that the behavior of your reel when you start fishing differs considerably from its behavior an hour or so later. An arbor of balsa wood, water-proofed with a coat or two of spar varnish, stays approximately the same weight all day long.

For a man who has plenty of time, it is often convenient and diverting to run down the intricacies of his own reel problems. For a busy man, however, this is usually out of the question. If you happen to be in the latter classification, your best bet is to put your faith in the manufacturers and buy a reel of good make with a dependable name and a reliable company behind it. That way, you are pretty sure to get what you want. A good reel costs more money than an average, fair reel, but it pays for itself over the years that you use it.

Your fly-rod reel is every bit as important a piece of equipment as your casting reel. Like casting reels, there are a great many bad fly-rod reels and a few good ones. Play safe and buy a good one. It may cost you twice as much at the start but twenty years later it still will be giving you good service.

A fly-rod reel serves three purposes. It carries the line that is not actually in use; it plays your fish safely and efficiently; and it *helps* to balance your rod. All three of its functions are important, so keep them all in mind when you are buying a new bass reel.

A bass fly line, when compared with the average trout

line, is a bulky affair. That being the case, your reel must be of a size that will accommodate this added bulk. Not only that, but you should allow for not less than one hundred yards of fairly stout "backing"—extra line, of either linen or silk or nylon, that will enable you to allow a large fish to use up his excess energy by completing his long runs. Then, too, it is not always possible for an angler to stop the determined run of a large fish. When a big bass—a really big one—gets the bit in his teeth and decides to go places, there is little to do about it but to hang on, applying enough pressure to make him work, and hope for the best. When your casting line vanishes from your reel drum, backing takes on all of the aspects of a parachute in a disabled airplane—there simply isn't any substitute. Without backing, matters arrange themselves into a tug of war and may the best man win. Usually in a case like this the best man is the bass. With backing, Mr. Bass can continue his run without doing any damage.

I find that the grilse reels make the most satisfactory bass reels. They are a bit large, but that, of itself, is a good fault. My Hardy "St. John" reel has an over-all diameter of three and seven-eighths inches and an over-all width of one and five-sixteenth inches. This reel comes equipped with a built-in metal arbor but there is still ample space for line and backing. The oversize diameter of the drum is an advantage, as one turn of the handle brings in almost a foot of line—a very important factor when you are playing a fish from the reel, which is how a fish should be played.

Grilse reels, as you know, are equipped with tension adjustments or "drags," which are used to place added pressure on a fighting fish. Make sure to choose a reel that places a *constant, unchanging* tension on the reel drum. Not all of them do this. Some reels, once the drums are in motion, place only moderate tension on the line, even though considerable force is required to start the drum once it has stopped. This results in a jerky, uneven release of the line, which is apt to give slack line to a fish if extreme care is not used.

The matter of the ratio of rod weight to reel weight reverts to the question of "balanced tackle." Some men like heavy reels; others like light reels; still others prefer no reels at all on the rods and have the reels attached to their belts. For my part, I believe that there should be a certain amount of moderation in all things. The accepted rule-of-thumb ratio is that the reel and line should be one and one half times the weight of the rod. My bass fly rods weigh slightly under seven ounces. According to that ratio, my reel should weigh not less than ten ounces. I usually carry three reel-and-line combinations with me and these weigh eight and one-half ounces, nine ounces, and nine and one-half ounces respectively. I'm still undecided as to which weight I prefer. Adding it all up, if your reel is not *too* heavy or *too* light, the matter of reel weight isn't really very important. My rods are equipped with long grips. On long casts my hand is back close to the reel so that I can utilize all of the rod's power and leverage. For casts of ordinary range, my hand is moved forward two or three inches. This change of position more than compensates for one or even two ounces of reel weight.

I suppose, since this chapter is devoted to the subject of bass reels, some mention should be made of other types than those that have been discussed. All right—let's take a quick look at the automatic reels. Automatic reels are all right if you like them. Frankly, I have no use for them. They are heavy, cumbersome, and impractical. And they don't allow you enough leeway in the matter of line and backing. Playing an average fish on an automatic reel is purely a matter of mechanics. Hold the rod and let the reel play the fish for you, tiring himself out against the unrelenting give and take of the spring-driven drum. That's one hell of a way to play a fish. And when you hook a big one, you are courting destruction. Most automatics do not have the capacity to carry both line and backing. And even if there is room, the spring tension won't let you use all of it. Sure, I know—some automatics can be thrown into free-spool. But that's a nuisance and a bit risky when you are playing a big fish. Then you have to re-engage the spring to reel in. You can have them. I'll stick to single-action grilse reels for my fly rods.

Then there's the spinning reel. Even the name of that one doesn't make any sense. These thread-line, fixed-spool, slip-cast affairs have been in use for a long time in Great Britain and Europe, I believe since Mr. H. Illingworth took out a patent on the idea in 1917. From what I can learn, his first reels were made by Malloch of Perth, Scotland. Somewhere in my archives I have what I believe to be the first Luxor reel to be brought to this country. It was given to me by Mr. Charles Ritz of Paris, France, in the fall of 1937.

Unquestionably, spinning, thread-line casting, slip-casting, call it what you will, is an easy way to cast light lures. For distances of thirty or forty feet an amateur can become an expert in half an hour, using a quarter-ounce lure. But—and here's the catch—at greater distances, say sixty to one hundred feet, complications set in. When the line is drawn off the end of the fixed spool at high speed, there is a "throw" exerted, at right angles to the direction of pull, which causes the line to rotate somewhat in the general plane of an oblate spheroid or football. This whirling motion must be condensed by the first guide on the rod. That is the reason for the oversize guide directly above the reel on a spinning rod. Naturally this sets up guide-and-line friction and cuts down distance.

Dick and I did some experimental work with spinning reels. I used the spinning reel and he used a straight quadruple multiplier, complete with level-winder. Using the same lures, which ranged from three-eighths to half an ounce, he could duplicate my best performances. Not only that—he wasn't using a light-lure reel, designed to handle quarter-ounce and five-eighth-ounce lures. Instead, he used a regular Pflueger "Supreme" which, as you know, functions best with five-eighth-ounce lures. As I say, he duplicated my best efforts and with a lot less fuss and exertion. Spinning reels, like automatics, are fine if you like them. They are easy to use and a beginner can learn to handle one effectively in no time at all, but a good caster, equipped with a light-lure outfit, can cast rings around any spinning outfit I have seen and I have four different kinds.

Most folks decline to give good reels the care they deserve, with the result that the reels don't give them the quality of performance for which they have been designed and for which the owner pays when he buys the reel. A reel should be cleaned thoroughly at least once a season and preferably twice. Remove the line, wash out the old grease with gasoline (better do this outdoors), and go over all the parts with an old toothbrush and a clean cloth. Then reassemble it, oil it thoroughly, and put it in a reel bag so that it won't pick up dust and grit. Before you use it, place a drop of oil on the moving parts and it will give you "new" performance for a long, long time. You don't need graphite in a reel. It's messy stuff, and good-quality, colorless reel oil will serve just as well. When this clear oil becomes black and foul, that's the danger signal. Dust and grit wear away your bushings almost like powdered emery, and loose bushings in a reel are indeed a sore trial. Take care of your reel. Then, when you are playing that lunker you have dreamed about, your reel will take care of you.

CHAPTER 6

Bass Lines and Leaders

For bass fishing, there are two materials that are generally accepted for use in line manufacture—silk and, more recently, nylon. The laid line of salt water finds no place for itself on fresh-water reels. Bass lines are braided, some round and some square, and therein lies a great deal of romance, background, and tradition of the sport of fresh-water angling. Just as rods, reels, and terminal tackle improved with passing years, so, naturally, did the design and quality of the lines that go with them.

There is neither need nor space here to go into the history of lines and their development to their present-day state of perfection. What concerns us now is the matter of selecting the right line for the task it must perform for us. As with other forms of tackle, you will do well to put your trust in the reliability of the manufacturer when you buy a line. No need to experiment. The line companies have done that for you. Their product is the result of many, many years of careful research and when you buy a six- or a nine- or a twelve-pound-test line, you can be fairly sure that you are getting what you pay for if the name on the box is that of one of the old, established houses.

Time was when the good casters insisted on lines of soft-braided silk. Some of these were braided around a core and some were not. For ease of casting, these old lines equaled our top-quality lines of today. But—backlash one of them, just once, and they snarled themselves around the reel drum in "bird nests" that frequently had to be cut free with a knife. Then, too, they wouldn't last. Each fishing trip took its toll in tensile strength and, if you were using one of low break test, it was sometimes necessary to "break back" the business end of your line during the day as a matter of safety. Even today, braided silk lines deteriorate rapidly, no matter how carefully you dry them after each use.

Most of the silk casting lines of today are waterproofed at the factory. This protects them to some extent from the ravages of use. Also, it makes them less flexible. Some new silk lines are processed to the extent that five or six inches of the end of the line will stand out without support, almost with no curve, when held parallel to the floor. This same waterproofing minimizes backlashes to some extent and renders the clearing of a backlash a fairly simple matter. But waterproofing or no, silk lines will lose their tensile strength with use.

The first nylon casting lines to appear on the market were not particularly satisfactory for use as casting lines. Nylon strands, as you probably know, will stretch at least 25 per cent of their length before they break. Those original lines of braided nylon not only would stretch the usual 25 per cent; the braiding added its effect so that one of them would lengthen out about one third more than its normal length before it let go. One of the manufacturers sent me a sample of these early nylon lines. It was packed in four connected spools, beautifully packaged, and labeled twelve-pound test. That was in 1938. I took it with me to Vermont that summer and with it I managed to lose one of the largest Smallmouth I ever saw, purely because I couldn't set the hooks. Next day at camp I wrapped the end of that line around Dick's finger

Bass Lines and Leaders

and then, holding the reel in my hand, paced off approximately one hundred feet. I called to Dick to hold his arm straight out from his shoulder, pointing the finger to which the line was fastened at right angles away from me. Then with the hand which held the reel I reached forward as far as I could, taking up line with the reel handle until the line was snug. This done, I swung my reel hand back away from Dick—hard—as far as I could reach. Dick's finger and arm did not so much as show any indication of changing their positions.

I still have most of that old line. Now it is used as backing on my fly-rod reels. For that purpose it is excellent, as it is strong and its elasticity automatically keeps tension on a running fish. But as a casting line it was a complete and absolute failure.

Today nylon lines are something else again. The line companies have learned to eliminate a great deal of that objectionable elasticity. They have evolved some method for pre-stretching the fibers of a braided line so that nearly all of the former stretch is gone. Nylon being quite strong, our light-lure lines can be set up in small diameters that have surprisingly high break tests. Only a few days ago, this same company sent me a sample of one of their new nylon spinning lines. It is square-braided and it measures approximately ten thousandths of an inch across its narrow diameter. While it is labeled five-pound test, I have been unable to break it with my bare hands, as the line will cut through the skin of my fingers before it shows any sign of breaking. In addition, almost all of the stretch has been taken out of it by the new braiding process. It is most surely the last word in casting lines.

Nylon has the added advantage of remaining unaffected by water. While the line, when in use, will take on in the folds of the braiding about 3 per cent of its weight in water, the material itself is not changed in any way. Thus nylon lines need not be removed from the reel and dried after use. And they retain their original tensile strength after a surprising amount of use. I've never had the bad luck to have a nylon line break while I was handling a heavy fish, but I have seen it happen. When the line lets go it sounds like a snapping fiddle string.

Casting ease increases as the diameter of the line is reduced. A nine-pound line casts easier than a twelve-pound line and a six-pound or a five-pound line casts easier than a nine-pound line. If you plan to cast five-eighth-ounce lures, the smaller diameters of the new lines make nine-pound or twelve-pound-test lines quite satisfactory. For light-lure work, the smaller diameters are better. Some men go as low as four-pound test, but such lines require careful handling when you are playing big fish.

Remember, a reel casts at top efficiency only when the drum is completely full of line, so that it just clears the pillars or spacer bars. Because of the fact that too much line on a reel spool takes on water, thereby adding weight and altering your reel action somewhat, it is unwise to have more than one hundred yards of line on the reel. It naturally follows that the arbor must take up the extra space. You can set in an arbor quite easily. All you need is two flat pieces of cork or balsa. Channel out the groove to fit around the spindle, using a "rattail" file. Shape the ends of the arbor with sandpaper to fit the contours of the end plates of the spool. Then rough out the shape of the arbor with a knife, and later a file, being sure to keep it slightly oversize. When the arbor has been fitted fairly snug, cement it to the shaft with Duco cement and, to ensure against slipping, place a drop or two on each end.

After the cement has set thoroughly, set the reel in a rod handle and fasten the rod handle in a vise, being sure to protect it from damage by wrapping it well with cloth. This done, get somebody to turn the reel handle for you, and

Bass Lines and Leaders

shape the arbor with strips of sandpaper. Once it is round, wind on your one hundred yards of line. By trial and error, you can gradually work the arbor down to size, using rough sandpaper at first and finishing the job with fine sandpaper or emery cloth. When the job is done, waterproof it with a coat or two of spar varnish. You can use a line dryer or an extra reel to hold your line for you while you are working the arbor down to the proper dimensions. It's an easy job that any angler can do.

Fly-rod lines, like casting lines, have kept pace with the general improvement in the quality of our tackle. Of course, for fly-rod use, you want a braided line that has been covered with an outside coat of dressing. Way back yonder, forty or forty-five years ago, when these lines first came out, they were called "enameled lines." Later on, after some of the British companies had developed oil finishes and "vacuum finishes," these enameled lines, in our particular group, were known as "linoleum lines." What lines they were! Until they were broken in by use, they came off the reel like watch springs. Having nothing else, however, we used them and were glad to get them.

The oil-finished and vacuum-finished lines were a big improvement but they had one universal failing—they would oxidize and become sticky or "tacky." Soakings in lime water, and subsequent polishings with powdered pumice, restored tacky lines to some extent, but the tung-oil finishes and present synthetic finishes are indeed a vast improvement on the original tapered lines that used to cost us from twelve to eighteen dollars apiece.

As with casting lines, two materials are used for braiding fly-rod lines—silk and nylon. After the lines have been braided, they are thoroughly impregnated with line dressing and then given several outside coats of the same dressing, each coat being dried before the next is applied. After the final coat

Black Bass

is applied, the lines are polished, usually with fine steel wool. Silk lines are appreciably heavier than nylon lines. Thus, for underwater lures, silk lines are the order of the day. For top-water lures, nylon is preferable by far. To give you some idea of comparative specific gravities, let us take the two extremes. The Ashaway "American Finish" line, which is built of braided silk with a heavy outside coat, has a specific gravity of 1.435. The Ashaway "Nylon" has a specific gravity of .98—two per cent lighter than water. Other makes go along somewhere between these two. I happen to know these gravities because I made it my business to find out by employing a New York laboratory to determine the specific gravities of eight different lines.

When it comes to the choice of line tapers, life was far simpler in the old days when we had only level lines for fly rods. Then there was little choice to make. We picked out what we hoped would be the right weight (usually it was far too light) and that was that. Today you really can go over-board when it comes to line tapers. No two companies have the same specifications. Neither are the gradings—A, B, C, D, and the like—exactly the same with any two line companies. One outfit, before World War II, carried in stock *thirty-two* different line tapers. That sort of business doesn't begin to make any sense.

In the first place, line sizes, by which tapers are identified, are supposed to be standardized. Size A, for instance, means that the line has a diameter of sixty thousandths of an inch. Size B is fifty-five thousandths; size C, fifty thousandths; size D, forty-five thousandths, and so on, down to size I, twenty thousandths.

All right, that's all very well in theory. Let's see how it works out in actual practice.

To understand the reason for variation in line sizes, you must remember how fly-rod lines are made. First, the body of the line is braided from silk or nylon strands, according to

Bass Lines and Leaders

size and desired taper. Then the braiding is impregnated with line dressing. When this is dry, coat after coat of line dressing is applied, gradually building up the diameter. Then the line is polished and this, in turn, reduces the diameter. With repeated additions and final subtraction, actual diameters are apt to be somewhat of a gamble. Some companies adhere rather closely to prescribed calibrations but others miss these measurements by a wide margin. Thus, when you buy a line that is identified, say, as HDH, it means, in theory, that this double taper is twenty-five thousandths of an inch at each end. The ends taper up through anywhere from eight to fourteen feet, depending on the company that made the line, to the main body or "belly" of the line which is size D, or forty-five thousandths of an inch in diameter. Actually, you are lucky if the diameters come within three or four thousandths of the true specifications, one way or the other. Most variations, however, are not smaller or larger than the true sizes.

With this size variation in mind, I practically disregard the A, B, C sizes when I'm buying a line, and guide myself with the readings on a micrometer. That way, I'm sure of what I am getting.

Up to a few years ago, most of us were satisfied with level lines or double tapers for our bass fishing. Then, about fifteen years ago, Marvin Hedge stepped up on the casting platform at the National Casting Tournament and proceeded to toss out a trout fly one hundred and seventy-six feet, breaking the world's record by approximately forty-five feet. Marvin had a line that was tapered and finished according to his own private specifications. It had a heavy forward section and a long taper called a "counterbalance," and it really turned out a casting job for Marvin.

Overnight, all and sundry began to experiment with triple- and quadruple-diameter lines. Before long the products of this experimentation began to appear on the tackle counters

Black Bass

under such names as "Torpedo-head Line," "Heavy-head Taper," "Three-diameter Line," "Distance Line," and so on. Some of them were usable lines while others were of such extreme design that casting them felt like throwing an apple off the end of a stick. If your timing was good, your back-cast was high, and you obeyed all the rules of casting, you could add not a little distance to your best efforts with an orthodox double taper, but if you made just one little error you were apt to find several skeins of fly line wrapped around your neck. These lines were designed for speed, with the result that the heavy forward end had an exceptionally fast turnover at the end of the cast. Unless extreme care was used, this fast turnover would put down a dry fly so hard that it actually would splash water when it struck the surface. It was almost impossible to lay down a light fly with one of the more extreme designs of "Torpedo-head" lines.

While these three-diameter affairs were not particularly important so far as the dry-fly fishermen were concerned, there were two main groups of anglers who found them of great benefit—the wet-fly anglers who fished for Atlantic Salmon on the East Coast and for Pacific Salmon and Steelhead on the West Coast, and the bass-bug fishermen. The Salmon fishermen, by adding distance to their casts, could cover a great deal more water. That, of course, helped, but they had had usable tackle prior to the advent of triple-diameters. But when the new designs came out in nylon braiding, the bass-bug men really hit the jack pot.

In the old days of bass-bug fishing, when our lines were built on braided silk, these lines were heavier than water. All that kept them afloat was the surface tension of the water, aided by liberal applications of line dressing. That way, they would float all right when they were first cast, but one or two twitches of the fly-rod tip, to set the bug in motion, would break the surface tension and down would go your

Bass Lines and Leaders

line. If there is any more annoying item in angling than a sinking line, when you want that line to float, I have yet to encounter it. To offset this inevitable sinking of our lines, we used to add extra flotation to the bugs themselves in the form of oversize cork or balsa heads. Deer-hair lures could be used only for a short time before they became completely waterlogged.

It so happened that nylon and three-diameter lines came into being at about the same time, and, of course, this material was used in braiding some of the new tapers. As I said before, nylon lines are slightly lighter than their equivalent bulk of water, at least they are when they are dry. This means that they will float without first being dressed with line grease. Of course, they get wet in a short time, take on a little water, and reach the point where they will no longer float, but even a soaked nylon line sinks very, very slowly. It is better, however, to dress every floating line with line dressing. It fills up the pores, waterproofs the line, and makes better use of surface tension. While fishing a lake or a pond on a sunny day, where there is no current to exert side pressure on your line, it is possible to fish with a dry line for hours on end. That is indeed God's blessing to the bass-bug fans.

In addition to improved flotation, the three-diameter lines brought with them several more benefits—increased distance of cast, added ease of handling a bass bug, and new facility for using more fragile, easily waterlogged lures. Almost overnight, deer-hair lures became quite practical.

But people—at least, people like me—are never satisfied. After using several of the new three-diameter tapers, I became convinced that we had not yet reached our final destination in fly-rod-line design. The tapers of most of these lines were much too extreme for practical, comfortable fishing. Some of them went so far as to grade down from sixty-three thousandths to thirty-two thousandths within the space of *four feet.* This quick taper was unable to dissipate the energy of the forward cast sufficiently for comfortable casting. The line would go out like a bullet, with an exceedingly tight bow, to turn over at the end of the cast with a decided snap. So I conceived the idea of utilizing the good features of both the torpedo-head lines and the old double tapers. For convenience, this combination was called the "forward taper." It worked out about like this:

At the front, or business end, of the line were two feet of level G. Then it tapered through eight feet to size A or size B, depending on the rod for which it was intended. Next came the heavy section or "belly" of size A or size B and this was thirty feet long. This, in turn, through a taper of ten feet, was reduced to a diameter of size F and this diameter was maintained to the rear end of the line—that which is fastened to the backing. Add a nine-foot leader to this forward assembly and the result is a line that casts and behaves exactly like a double taper. It does not require the last word in timing, it throws a tight or a wide bow, as you wish, and it handles readily in curve casts. When you want extra distance—and you always do when you are fishing a bass bug— the light F running line greatly facilitates the ease of shoot. In short, it is a double-taper line with the rear taper moved *forward* to the center of the line—hence, "forward taper." With it you can fish any sort of bass bug you want to use, with the assurance that you can place that bug accurately and lightly and keep it reasonably dry the while. I have several of these lines and they are by far the most satisfactory I have been able to find.

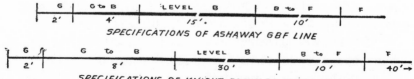

SPECIFICATIONS OF ASHAWAY GBF LINE

SPECIFICATIONS OF KNIGHT FORWARD-TAPER LINE

Bass Lines and Leaders

"Spinning" lines or "slip-casting" lines, if you insist on using these reels, are of three basic types—braided silk, braided nylon, and continuous strands of raw nylon or of "Japanese gut." If you are using nonspinning lures, you probably will like the braided nylon lines, but if you are addicted to spinning lures, which will twist and kink your line, no matter how many swivels you tie in, then the raw nylon is preferable. "Japanese gut" or "synthetic gut" would be just about as good if it were not for the nuisance of keeping it wet.

In the matter of leaders, your choice, with a few exceptions, has been simplified greatly for you since the introduction of nylon. There are only a few times during the course of a season when nylon strands won't do the job for you. Not that nylon is the be-all and end-all in leader materials. It isn't. But for most uses in angling for bass, it serves the purpose very well.

The easy way to attach a leader to a fly-rod line

While we are at it, let's take a close look at nylon strands, as there are some things about them that an angler should know.

In the first place, nylon changes its characteristics somewhat at various temperatures. Sure, I know that the manufacturers say it doesn't and we have had some correspondence about that very thing. But they are basing their contention on laboratory tests and theory while I am basing mine on field experience—sad, very sad experience. If there is one thing connected with the sport of fresh-water angling with which I have little patience or tolerance it is leader failure. We pay, goodness knows, plenty of money for leaders. There is no reason why we shouldn't get what we pay for. Yet we seldom do, particularly in leaders that taper down into the "x" sizes. That goes for both nylon and silkworm gut. For instance, you buy a nice new nylon leader. You take it with you on the opening day of the trout season, still coiled in its pretty envelope. When you assemble your tackle, you un-coil this nice new leader, attach it to your line and, if you are a prudent angler, test it for weak spots from one end to the other. All well and good. Then you cast that leader into water, the temperature of which is in the high thirties or low forties. In due course, you hook a fish that is heavy enough to subject that leader to some strain—not excessive strain, mind you, but just an ordinary pull that is expected in such circumstances. For that matter, if you keep your rod well up while you are fighting a fish it requires a good deal of effort and not a little strain on the rod to exert a pressure of two pounds on the leader. I'm talking about a fly rod now, not a casting rod. Try it sometime against a spring scale and you'll see. All right— you're exerting only normal strain on that leader when suddenly, for no evident reason, your line goes slack. It's a sickening sensation. You reel in and find that your nice new leader has parted company, not at one of the knots but right smack in the middle of a strand. Naturally you are puzzled. You tested the leader not ten minutes earlier, while it was still dry, and warm from being in your pocket, and it was all right. What happened? I'll tell you. Nylon, in the high-thirty, low-forty temperature range, becomes slightly brittle, and light leader strands will fracture all too easily in these temperatures. Five different times in the past eight or nine years I have allowed myself to be talked into using nylon leaders in the cool waters of early season. Each time the story has been the same—I've lost a nice fish through leader failure.

Of course, you don't find low water temperatures during the early-season bass fishing, but you do in October and November, so keep that little point in mind.

Bass Lines and Leaders

All right, let's go to the other extreme. In the hot weather, nylon tends to soften up slightly and lose some of its bounce and resiliency. I realize that I'll get an argument on this, too, but the fact remains that nylon being fished in eighty-five degree water (and some of our bass fishing is done at those temperatures) loses some of its rigidity, with the result that a leader of that material does not turn over well at the end of a long cast. Sure, it's strong enough when the weather is warm, but it does become "slimpsy." (In case you don't know that one, that's Pennsylvania for droopy, soft, extrapliable.)

However, there is a cure for these things. Size for size, nylon is stronger than gut in the larger diameters. Thus, in cold weather, use either oversize nylon or fine gut leaders. In warm weather, extra diameter will provide added resiliency; use oversize diameters in your hot-weather leaders too.

For a casting rod, I prefer a leader that is long enough to allow a few inches between rod tip and lure and still allows one or two turns on the reel drum. Some anglers advocate fifteen or twenty feet of leader, claiming that the long leader cuts down guide friction at the beginning of the cast. I guess it really doesn't make much difference but depends on what you happen to like. I carry in my kit coils of nylon strands that calibrate from ten to twenty-two thousandths of an inch. That way I have free range in the matter of leaders, regardless of the size of the line or the lure I happen to be using.

For fly-rod use, regardless of the type of lure, I prefer a tapered leader because it casts better than a level one, it turns over better. Unless I happen to be fishing light deer-hair lures, my usual bass-bug leader will be about ten or twelve feet long, tapered from twenty thousandths down to thirteen or fourteen thousandths of an inch. I find that four feet of twenty thousandths, three feet of eighteen, three feet of sixteen, and a tippet of fourteen or thirteen thousandths casts nicely and turns over a bass bug or a streamer very well at the end of a long cast. As I say I carry a good supply of nylon

Black Bass

strands in my kit and I can tie what leaders I need as I want them. In hot weather, unless conditions call for ultralight tackle, I use diameters that are slightly larger than normal. Of course, when we are fishing waters where there are plenty of snags, then I cut down on length and use larger, stronger strands so that extra pressure can be exerted to hold a fish out of trouble.

KEY TO BASS-BUG COLOR PLATE

KNIGHT BULLDOZER	KNIGHT MYSTERY BUG (SMALLMOUTH)	KNIGHT MYSTERY BUG (LARGEMOUTH)
E. H. PECKINPAUGH'S MARTIN POPPING MINNOW	PECK'S T.V.A. POPPING MINNOW	WILDER-DILG FEATHER MINNOW
HEDDON POP EYE FROG	Z. D. BROWN'S PRAIRIE DU CHIEN BUG	HARNDEN'S BROOKS SPOUTER
TOM LOVING'S GERBUBBLE BUG	HARVEY HARNDEN'S BALTIMORE POPPER	JOHN SCOTT'S AMPHISBAENA

KEY TO COLOR PLATE OF HAIR BUGS

BUBB'S DEER-HAIR BEETLE

JOE MESSINGER'S POPPING
GOLDEN FROG

MESSINGER POPPING
NITE HUMMER

JOE MESSINGER'S MEADOW FROG

VARIANT OF STURGIS MOTH

ROY YEATS' THE DEACON

WEAVER FROG

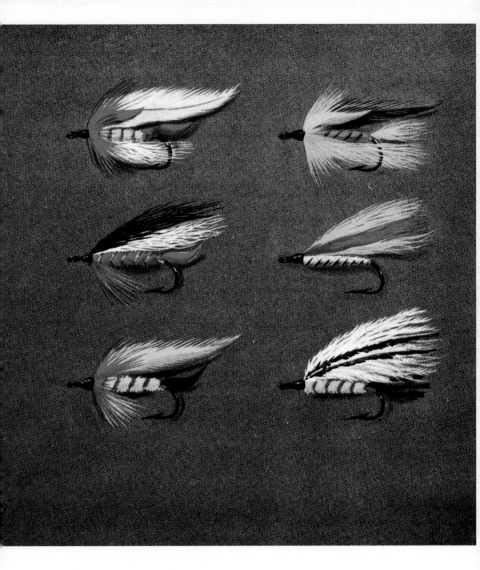

KEY TO COLOR PLATE OF BASS STREAMERS

KNIGHT'S DELAWARE   KNIGHT'S BROWN BOMBER

FRANK COOPER   KNIGHT'S MICKEY FINN

CHALKY BAUDER   JOHN WOODHULL'S MARABASS

CHAPTER 7

Bass Lures

▲▲

WHEN DISCUSSING BASS lures, it is possible to deal only in the vaguest of generalities. Pick up any tackle catalogue or outdoor magazine and the reason is quite evident. There are literally thousands upon thousands of bass lures now on the market. To single out one or several of these not only would savor of discrimination but, after all, would be only one man's opinion. The whole truth of the matter is that bass, when they are hungry and on the feed, will sample anything that moves and looks even remotely edible. Just to see what would happen, some years ago, when we lived in Florida, we tried the fascinating stunt of making odd, fantastic lures, using for materials anything that happened to come to hand. We used clothespins, unadorned save with hooks and still *looking* like clothespins; we used bottle tops, still round and with fluted edges; we used round cork floats, kitchen spoons, Christmas-tree trimmings of tinsel, balsa-wood chunks, anything. The only rule was that its true shape must not be altered and it must not be painted. Otherwise there were no restrictions. While we did not catch many bass on any one of these concoctions, we *did* catch *some* bass on each and every one of them, no matter how insane it looked to us. As a matter

93

of fact, back around 1930 the winning Largemouth in the Southern Division was taken from the Mosquitoe River in Florida on a lure made from a wooden saltcellar—the sort that used to sell for a dime in the five-and-ten.

It should not be concluded that all bass lures are good bass lures merely because they happen to take bass when the fish are on the feed. Some lures unquestionably are better than others. Well-known popular lures do not become famous solely because their makers conduct intensive advertising campaigns. Regardless of what the manufacturers have to say about them, these lures must produce fish consistently if they are to continue to be favorites among the bass fishermen. Thus, if you see that a lure *continues* to be featured prominently in the advertising pages of our outdoor publications year after year, you can be safe in assuming that such a lure will do what you expect it to do when you use it.

Bass plugs, to qualify as good ones, should have several desirable attributes in addition to "fish appeal." Let's take a look at the critical qualities that determine whether a bass plug is a good one or a bad one.

In the first place, a bass plug should be sturdily built so that it will give lasting service. The early bass plugs were made of red cedar, as this wood does not take on water and expand. Expansion will crack the finish; this is to be avoided at all costs. The line ring and the hooks were hung on with simple screw eyes, the plug was painted and trimmed, and that was that. It didn't take very long for the threads that anchored the screw eyes in the body of the plug to become tired with use. Hooks on old plugs were always pulling out.

Today the fittings on a plug are put on to stay. No longer does the hook exert direct pull on the threads of the fittings, and the anchorages are so arranged that the hooks can not become tangled with each other. Plastics are being used more and more extensively and some plugs have hook anchorages

Bass Lures

and line ring all built into a solid metal skeleton about which the plug is built. These plugs can really take it and give almost unlimited service.

A bass plug should be neatly finished and trimmed in a pattern that appeals to fish. There are four or five more or less standard finishes, such as the red head and white body, the frog finish, the chub finish, the perch finish, and so on. Recently it has been learned that orange and black or dark brown seems to have great appeal for fish. Some of the manufacturers are capitalizing on this, but mostly fishermen will buy the old standard finishes in preference to something new.

Fishermen's preferences must be taken into account as well as fish preferences in the manufacture of lures. Some years ago I did some experimenting with colors, and I found that blue—almost any shade of blue—will take bass to beat the band. Some of my best catches in the Delaware have been taken on blue and white combinations and on two shades of blue. Yet it's a safe bet that a blue plug would sit on the shelf of a tackle shop from now until kingdom come. All white and all black are good too, but they don't sell as well as the accepted standard finishes.

Another important factor in bass-plug design is what might be termed its "castability." In other words, its weight-to-air-resistance ratio should be such that the plug will move away from the reel readily, maintaining tension on the line, not wavering on its course, and casting true to the spot at which it is aimed. This sort of castability eliminates backlashes and shore-line complications and makes for easy, pleasant casting. One of the best fish-getting plugs on the market has its sale and its use greatly retarded purely because it is such a miserable thing to cast.

The great majority of the bass plugs weigh five-eighths of an ounce. This seems to be the weight that lends itself best to easy handling. Most casting reels are built for the handling of five-eighth-ounce lures, and the majority of the casting rods are designed for this weight. Recently the tendency has been toward lighter, smaller lures—half ounce, three-eighth or quarter ounce—but the big sale still holds in five-eighth-ounce tackle. To cast small lures satisfactorily you need light-lure tackle and that means buying a complete extra casting outfit, all of which runs into money.

Last, but by no means least, a plug should handle well and have "fish appeal." This last item is a vague, indeterminate thing, difficult to define. The action of a plug in the water or on top of it is something that is not decided upon casually by the manufacturers. The actions of two plugs may seem to us to be almost identical, yet one will catch fish consistently and the other will not. Why this is so I'm not prepared to say, but it certainly is true. For this reason, before a plug is placed on the market by one of the big companies, it is tested exhaustively under actual fishing conditions. When you are buying bass plugs, better keep that in mind.

Another thing—good hooks are just as important on a bass plug as they are anywhere else. Always try to find bass plugs that are equipped with hollow-point hooks. There is no question about the superior penetrating quality of these as compared with file-point or spear-point hooks. And hollow-point hooks are so much easier to keep needle-sharp.

HOLLOW POINT   SPEAR POINT

The two types of hook points

Bass Lures

Plugs come in three general categories—deep-running plugs, shallow-running plugs, and surface lures or floaters. These all have their very definite uses and your kit should be well equipped with all three varieties.

The metal lures also come in three general classes— spoons, spinners, and wobblers. The spoons, as you know, are designed to revolve or rotate independent of aid. The spinners, for their rotation, depend upon being held at a fixed angle, usually furnished by a shaft. The wobblers or "flutterers" do what their names suggest and do not rotate if they are properly made. These metal lures, like the plugs, are legion in number. For fishing in the weeds or in places liberally sprinkled with snags, stumps, and brush piles, they are usually more practical than the plugs. As a rule, their effectiveness is increased by the addition of a rubber "hula skirt" or a strip of pork rind. Incidentally, instead of using an attracter of these synthetic materials, did you ever try cutting a similar strip from the belly of a fresh-caught bass and using that instead of pork rind? You'd be surprised. There is something about the smell of fresh meat that seems to build up their effectiveness immensely. These strips are not as durable as pork rind (few things are) but they surely do take fish.

Some rigs are designed expressly for the use of pork rind and pork chunk. Properly handled, these lures are just about as deadly as anything you can cast into fresh water, particularly when fishing for Largemouth. Of course, you can buy pork rind and pork chunks all nicely cut and put up in bottles of preservative, but while it is a messy job, fresh-cut pork rind or pork chunks seem to take more fish. There must be something about the odor or taste of the fresh pork that does it. I don't know, frankly. But the fact remains that the fresh-cut lures do seem to be more effective. These, too, will do great slaughter among the weeds, rushes, and snags whereas a plug, no matter how "weedless," will give you nothing but trouble in the same waters.

Fly-rod fishing for bass, when compared to casting-rod fishing, is lagging in general appeal. However, it is gaining rapidly in popularity. While I realize that there are many who will give me an argument on this, I am firmly convinced that a bass bug, properly cast and correctly handled or played (and these qualifications are vitally important) is the most deadly bass lure yet to be contrived by man. Today it is possible to purchase an unlimited variety of bass bugs (and this was not true as recently as 1940) but for some reason it is difficult to find good usable bugs in the tackle shops. Most of them literally aren't fit to carry with you.

A bass bug, to be a *good* bass bug, must have several essential qualities. First and foremost, it must cast well—handle easily with a long line. This means that it must have the correct weight-to-air resistance ratio. That's another way of saying that it must be heavy enough so that its inertia, when in motion, *almost* equalizes the drag it sets up by its air resistance. Take a look at the two extremes. The fluffy, loosely tied deer-hair bugs, with the wings jutting out from the sides, are so light in weight and have so much air resistance that it is all a man can do to turn one of them over at the end of a long cast, even on a still day. To attempt to cast one of these powderpuffs into a wind—or a light breeze—is just about impossible. Conversely, the little flat spoons and wobblers, some of which are shaped like little fish, are so heavy (comparatively) and have so little air resistance that they are the devil's own job to cast well. These things exert little or no pull on the leader while they are in motion. Thus, they are always trying to get ahead of the timing of the cast. They drop too fast at the end of the backcast and they turn over at the end of the forward cast long before the slack line has completed its shoot—that is, they do unless care is taken to

Bass Lures

throw a great wide bow, with the timing of the cast advanced considerably ahead of normal casting timing. Sure, they can be cast, but it's a very specialized job to cast them well and accurately at distances greater than forty or fifty feet. The happy medium—the well-made bass bug—is just heavy enough *almost* to carry itself as it travels through the air on the cast, exerting only enough resistance against the line to keep the leader straight. At the end of the forward cast, this sort of bug will "turn over" easily, straightening the leader and coming to rest on the water without too much disturbance.

Once on the water, the bug should play well. It should float high, not awash. Bass seem to prefer bugs that float high up on the surface. When agitated by twitching of the rod tip or jerking on the line, it should kick up a satisfactory fuss in the water without skipping or pulling under. Thus, the face must be carefully designed. Beware of bugs that are made with concave cups in their faces or long lips that protrude from the lower parts of their heads. They are a constant headache to the long caster. Good bugs are made with convex faces and *rounded edges*. These make enough disturbance on the surface and will "pop" with the best of them. In addition, they will pick up with any length of line without diving, and will travel through the air in a straight line so that there is no loss in accuracy. A bug that is improperly designed will dive on the pickup and is a constant threat to your rod tip.

Cork head of a Mystery Bass Bug. Note rounded edges.

Added to all this, a bass bug should resemble or suggest some small creature on which the bass feed—an injured insect or a small animal, bird, frog, or minnow. We know that

99

Black Bass

a bass, if he happens to be in a striking mood, will hit almost anything that moves, but if the bug has some semblance of familiar edibility, it usually will produce better than one that looks like nothing the fish has ever seen before.

As with plugs, be sure to get bass bugs that are built on top-quality, hollow-point hooks. They are easy to keep sharp and they will save a lot of fish for you. The eyes of the hooks on bass bugs should be straight-ringed eyes, not turned down or turned up. The reason for this is quite obvious if you think about it a bit. A bass bug should be fished slowly. This means that the leader is bound to sink. If the bug has a turned-down or turned-up eye, the downward pull of the leader tends to pull the bug under. However, if the bug has a straight-ringed eye, and if the leader is introduced *from the under side* and tied on with a Turle knot, the pull of the leader tends to tip up the face of the bug and keep it playing on the surface. Some of the companies already recognize this fact but most of them still use turned-down eyes.

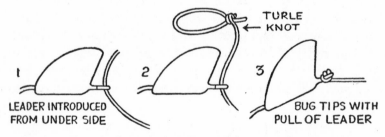

How to tie a leader to a bass bug with a straight-ringed eye

Probably there never will be any agreement on the matter of color. Some folks prefer bright, flashy colors; others prefer to have their colors subdued. About all that can be done is to generalize. And, strangely enough, the rules that apply to plugs do not necessarily hold good with bass bugs.

Most of the time, color in a bass bug is not very important.

Bass Lures

Every now and again, however, the bass show a decided preference, rising readily to a certain color and refusing to look at others. When we journeyed to North Carolina to see what we could find out about the brackish-water bass in the waters of Currituck and Albemarle, we took with us a wide selection of bass bugs. After a great deal of experimentation, we learned that the bass of that section showed a decided leaning toward yellow. To make sure, we subjected the yellow bugs to the most severe tests. One of us would fish along a shore line with a white bug or a brown bug. Following not a hundred feet behind the first boat, the second angler would fish a yellow bug over the same water, casting pretty much in the same spots. Of course the first boat would take some bass, but the second boat, with the yellow bug, would take even more. Should the position of the boats be reversed, the yellow bug would take so many bass that the second boat, using another color, would find almost no takers. This condition continued not only throughout the entire week that we fished those waters, but on several subsequent trips to that same area.

Here's another strange thing about that fishing. In our northern lakes and rivers, the little Messinger hair frog is just about as deadly a lure as a man can find for use with the fly rod. Largemouth or Smallmouth—it makes no difference. Those little hair frogs really produce in most waters. Yet in the brackish waters of eastern North Carolina they were practically useless. It may be that there are no frogs in the salt marshes. I'm not sure. At all events, after many hours of fruitless casting I reluctantly put my frogs back in my kit and left them there.

I'm a firm believer in white as a color for bass bugs. Of course, white isn't a color, but I have raised hundreds and hundreds of bass, of both varieties, to all-white bugs. Conversely, a friend of mine fishes almost exclusively with bugs that are solid jet black, and he always catches his share of bass.

Black Bass

Red makes a good color for trim, but I don't care for all-red lures. Brown seems to be good—natural brown, such as deer hair or natural, unpainted cork—yet painted brown never seems to produce the way it should. One of the best patterns I know is an unpainted cork head with a shawl of white bucktail. A tackle dealer wouldn't dare to place such a lure on his counter for sale but the fact remains that with one bass hook, one bottle cork, a piece of strong silk thread, and a pinch of white bucktail you can make a lure that will catch bass with the best of them.

On one color alone there seems to be some agreement. That color is green. Never have I met a bass fisherman who wants any green in his bass flies or bugs. Yet the plug fishermen use green plugs—frog finish, chub finish, and so on—and swear by them.

Just as is the case with plugs, blue is seldom used in trimming bass flies and bugs. This is strange as blue is an excellent color for bass. As stated earlier, I used to tie a bass streamer of white and blue, plenty of blue, and it took bass for me as well as most of the good flies and far better than the average.

Of late years orange seems to be gaining in popularity. One tackle company goes so far as to state, outright, that an orange plug is the number-one killer among artificial baits. All right—add up this one. Try as I will, I can't catch fish on a brown and orange bass bug or an orange and yellow bug or an all-orange bug. I've tried them all—repeatedly and at length—and for me they just will not produce. The more I try to find out about color, the less I seem to know.

While bass bugs are, for me at least, the most pleasant to use and the most productive of the fly-rod lures, there are other lures that are equally important. Take the little metal gadgets such as the Trixoreno, the Tin Lizz, the double-ought Drone, pearl wobblers, Dardevil, Johnson Minnow, and such. These little things are difficult to cast, but there is no

Bass Lures

question as to their fish-taking ability. Theirs is the virtue of being able to go down after the fish when surface lures are being ignored.

In the brackish waters of North Carolina, there were times when the bass were not on the shore lines. Then we would fish the double-ought Drones, casting them out across the passes and thoroughfares with long lines and letting them sink to the bottom. These little lures seldom failed to produce bass for us.

The first fly-rod lures for bass were "bass flies." These were nothing more than oversize trout flies in the standard patterns—Professor, Royal Coachman, Brown Hackle, and so on. They were tied with heavy snells, usually double ones, and on #1 or #2 regular-shank hooks. They caught bass but not well enough to be considered the last word in fly-rod lures. Long before such things as bass streamers were manufactured for sale (as a matter of fact the word "streamer" did not come into use until E. R. Hewitt developed streamer flies for trout in 1928 or 1929) I began to experiment with streamers. The first one, concocted in 1919, I called Old Glory. It was a fearsome-looking affair with a red chenille body, gold rib, blue hackle and tail. Extending back from the head—one on top, one on each side, and one on the bottom— were four long white saddle hackles which terminated an inch or so beyond the end of the short tail. Believe it or not, this fly actually took bass so much better than standard bass flies that I discarded the latter completely. Later, of course, came the bass streamers and bucktails as we know them today, but I really believe that bass streamers, dressed in the fashion of the original Old Glory, will hold their own with the best present-day patterns.

A great many bass fishermen, instead of using streamers and bucktails by themselves, prefer to fish them fastened to some sort of a spinner rig. As you know, there are all sorts of spoons and spinners on the market. Some of these are practical and satisfactory for fly-rod use; by far the large majority of them literally are not worth hell-room. That's what makes me impatient with so many of our tackle manufacturers. They waste so much effort and good material in turning out lures that have not been properly engineered. This matter of fly-rod spinners is a fine example of faulty design.

We know, if we have so much as been exposed to elementary physics, that a flat plate is the least stable of all forms when passing through a liquid. Bend it into a curve and it tends to find a static, balanced position for itself when it is forced through a liquid. Thus a spinner, to be completely unstable—in other words, to be sure to spin—should be as flat as possible. Yet by far the great majority of fly-rod spinners are made with a deep curve to the spoon proper. All right, that's point number one.

Unless you want to twist your leader into knots, your fly-rod spinners should be mounted free-blade, with a saddle and a wire shank. If you buy a fixed-angle spinner (one that is held in position by a small bracket, such as the June Bug spinner) the friction of the bearings against the shank is going to put twists into your leaders and line unless you use swivels which add weight. If you use the Colorado mounting (swivel and split ring) once more you are in for trouble with a twisted leader. With the free-blade mounting, however, you can rest assured that you will have no trouble of this sort providing the spoon is working correctly.

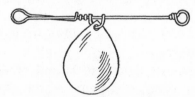

Probably the best of the fly-rod spoons, designed for use with a streamer fly

Bass Lures

In addition to dependable performance, you want two other qualities built into your spoon. You want the maximum amount of light flashes for the minimum amount of weight and you want the maximum r.p.m. (revolutions per minute) for the minimum forward motion. To arrive at these two results, you should have a spoon that revolves at an angle of not less than forty-five degrees from the line of the shank. After fooling around with Willowleaf, Kidney, Colorado, Fluted Skinner, Indiana, and Montreal shapes, not to mention a conglomeration of odds and ends, I gave up and had my own die made. This die stamps out a spoon of Colorado shape, but instead of being deeply dished, it is almost flat with just a slight cup at the end farthest away from the shank. This blade is nine sixteenths of an inch wide and three quarters of an inch long. It is stamped from tempered brass stock, thirteen thousandths of an inch thick. The maximum depth of the "dish" is thirty-six thousandths of an inch—this at the base of the "cup" at the end of the blade. Without doubt, this blade will out-perform any of the commercial blades that have come to my notice. In all fairness, why can't the average manufacturer of fishing tackle take time to find out how to make a good blade instead of putting out second-grade stuff that makes it necessary for interested individuals to go to all that trouble and expense if they want satisfactory equipment?

Here's another thing to remember about free-blade spoons. The rate of spin is in direct ratio to the distance that the blade is hung from the shaft. Therefore, buy a rig that has a small saddle which allows only a few thousandths of an inch clearance between the shank and the blade. Spoons that are hung on oversize saddles spin comparatively slowly.

Just as yellow seems to be an attractive color to bass, a gold-finish spoon seems to be best for all-round use. To be sure, the nickel blades get results, as do copper blades, but I find that gold-finish is entirely satisfactory.

There is one more type or group of fly-rod lures that

should be mentioned—the fly-rod plugs. These, as the name suggests, are miniature versions of the full-size plugs for use with the casting rod. Naturally, these miniatures came into being after the development of their big brothers—probably around 1912 or 1915.

There is no question about the fish-taking ability of the fly-rod plugs, providing, of course, that they are properly designed. One in particular, the fly-rod Flatfish, has set up a tremendous record for itself. However, I don't like them. The little heavy ones that are designed for deep fishing will take bass to beat the band, especially big Smallmouth, when the summer sun is hot and the fish lie in the deeper, cooler water. But they, like the metal fly-rod lures, are mean things to cast and not much fun to fish. The ones that float on the surface are not, in my biased opinion, as effective as bass bugs. By and large, I can take my fly-rod plugs or leave them alone, preferably the latter.

Every now and then a new lure is introduced that is represented to be the cure-all for the angler's ills—the perfect lure that will take fish any old time of day or night, spring, summer, and fall. For a while you hear a great deal about this lure. Everybody buys one and takes fish on it. Then, gradually, its taking quality seems to fall off and it may take its place in your kit as a good standard lure, no better and no worse than many others. Just as often, it is popular for a few seasons and then is forgotten.

The probabilities are that new lures, if they are well designed, take fish well purely because they are new. Not all bass are susceptible to the same designs or the same colors. Some like white lures, others like black, and others yellow or what have you. Some go for wobblers, some for darters, some for large lures, some for small ones. Most of our bass waters are fished rather thoroughly these days. Thus, when something different shows up, it is bound to find some takers to which its particular design happens to appeal. Sooner or

Bass Lures

later, however, its effectiveness generally tapers off. Experiments at some of the hatcheries show that this is true. It's a good idea to have a wide selection in your kit. Then you will be prepared to meet conditions as you find them.

CHAPTER 8

Incidental Equipment

I SUPPOSE EVERY bass fisherman, if he goes in for artificial-bait fishing, has his tackle box in which he carries his reels and his terminal tackle. That is standard equipment, particularly for the plug caster. But there are other items, in addition to the tackle box and terminal tackle, that can do with a little discussion.

For instance, what kind of a hook hone do you carry? Most of the ones on sale at the tackle stores are fast-cutting affairs, usually of carborundum. While they will sharpen a hook in a hurry, they do take off quite a bit of metal. My preference is one of the finer, slower-cutting stones, such as the toolmakers use. To be sure, they require a little more time, but the finished job is smooth, keen, and more effective. In addition, your hooks will last longer with fine stones.

Another handy item in a bass kit is a pair of good pliers—small ones, equipped with a wire cutter of the blade type.

Instead of letting your swivels, casting weights, snaps, extra guides, split rings, odd hooks, and so on rattle around loose in one of the compartments of your tackle box, try carrying them compactly in little metal boxes, the sort that your druggist uses to put up salve. That way they won't rust and you can always find them.

Incidental Equipment

Nowadays, instead of buying your nylon leader material in coils, you can buy it in flat plastic holders where it can't become tangled and is always ready for use.

Another useful item is a coil of stainless-steel wire that can be used for leaders, casting traces, or to "de-weed" a bass bug, or a pork-rind or pork-chunk rig.

Something you don't need often but which you do need in earnest when the time comes is a small emergency kit. I carry a very compact one. In it is a small box of aspirin, a few bandaids, a small bottle of "hospital mercurochrome," and a roll of one-inch bandage. This kit takes up very little room and will pay for its space in the box many, many times.

Then, too, you will want a foot rule and a portable scale to measure and weigh your fish. Perhaps the best compromise is the "De-Liar." This little gadget is compact and accurate and entirely practical.

If you fish from a boat, there are two items that really are necessities—a stringer and a boat cushion. We use the "keep-'em-alive" stringer, with the individual clips. This takes up very little space and it will keep your fish in good condition until the day is over. Instead of spending a lot of money on expensive boat cushions, we use the small rubber cushions that fold or roll compactly to fit into most any bait box. They cost only about fifty cents and last a surprisingly long time.

For boat fishing, the collapsible landing net is about the handiest. When not in use, it folds into a compact case and takes up little space in the car.

One of the handiest gadgets that a boat fisherman can carry is a sponge, either a natural one or a plastic one. No matter how careful you are, your shoes are bound to bring into the boat some sand or mud from shore, and there is nothing worse for lines and tackle. A sponge will clean this up in a jiffy. A bailer will take out most of the rain water in

Black Bass

the bottom of the boat, but a sponge will pick up the last drop. For cleaning and drying seats and floor boards it is ideal. It is easy to carry and it will pay for itself many times over in the course of a season.

For fishing the smaller bass rivers, we prefer to wade. For years we kidded ourselves that "wading wet" was the most comfortable plan for summer weather, but we finally gave up that nonsense in favor of waders. Wading wet is comfortable only during the warm hours of the day. When the sun goes down, you have the choice of changing into dry clothes or freezing on the way home. If you wish to change location during the day, the seat cushions in the car are bound to get wet.

With waders, you stay dry. Sure, they are hot if you do much walking, but along a bass river that usually isn't necessary. If you want to go someplace in the car, merely slip your waders down around your knees and the seat cushions don't suffer. And when evening comes, off comes the waders, on go the shoes, and you are dry and comfortable on the way home.

We use the stocking-foot waders and the hobnailed wading brogues. It takes a little more time to get into these than it does the boot-foot type but the added stability, once you have them on, is well worth the trouble.

Felt soles are all right if you like them, but I'll take hobnails. Every year I have quite a few guests who come to fish. Most of them, goodness knows why, bring felt-soled shoes with them. They get along all right so long as things are normal, but if the streams are a bit high and the going a little rough, I spend a great deal of my time acting as an animated wading staff, seeing to it that the felt-sole boys stay right side up. My hobs will hold on slippery rocks and in heavy water where felt soles are completely useless. In addition, felt soles wear out much too quickly for fellows who fish as much as we do.

For complete independence, the portable boat and small outboard are ideal.

This portable boat draws about two inches of water and handles beautifully.

Joe Brooks, of Baltimore, fishing a bass bug along the shore lines of Currituck Sound, North Carolina.

Incidental Equipment

Unless the weather is really tropical, we wear wool to fish in, wool pants and light wool shirts. Wool doesn't take up so much condensation as cotton and it keeps you warm. That, of course, is a matter of personal preference, but we fish a lot more than most folks and we find it the most practical.

For wading, we strip down to the barest essentials in gear. When the weather is warm, we don't use fishing jackets. In our wader pockets we can carry all the terminal tackle we need. For bait casting, there is plenty of space in the pocket for three or four extra plugs, and for fly-rod fishing a compact fly box will carry all the extra bass bugs, streamers, and so forth, that we can use.

For creels, we use either the flat, woven-grass creels or flat wicker creels, curved to fit the body. Orthodox wicker creels are too bulky for comfort. The landing net is hung from the ring of the creel harness, held in place by a "French snap" such as are used on dog leashes. A small can of line dressing and extra nylon leaders can be carried in the creel. Light nylon rain jackets fit nicely into the wader pockets. That is about all you need for wading gear, and you are not burdened by a hot fishing jacket.

For more years than I like to contemplate, I put up with the inconvenience of depending upon boat liveries. Some of the craft in which we have fished for bass literally weren't fit to be chopped up for kindling wood, as they were too waterlogged to burn. Then, too, the demand for boats all too often exceeds the supply. By and large, rented boats are an acute pain in the neck.

We decided that it would be a good idea to buy a portable boat. We had our own ideas about what a portable boat should be. After looking over the market pretty thoroughly, we found it. The one we have is twelve feet long, square ended, flat bottomed, and stable enough to stand up in safely. It has a forty-inch beam and a thirteen-inch freeboard. When

Black Bass

I'm in it alone, it draws about two inches of water. It is made of aluminum and weighs seventy-six pounds. I can load it onto the carrying racks on top of my car by myself without any trouble, and loading or unloading doesn't take more than five minutes.

Now we can go bass fishing without worrying about boats. We fish where we please and in comfort. Our boat is always clean and dry. Sometimes we take two cars, parking one well downstream from our starting point, so that we can fish several miles of river instead of having our activities localized because of rented boats. Not only that, but we can reach places that are seldom if ever fished. The big river scows that are standard equipment on the North Branch of the Susquehanna weigh anywhere from five hundred pounds to half a ton. I mean that, literally. They are huge, bulky things, watersoaked and unbelievably heavy. To attempt to take one of them through fast water is a back-breaking undertaking. With our light little portable, we can negotiate most fast-water areas. The white-water rapids can be by-passed by walking along shore and floating the boat through the shallows. Empty, it draws less than one inch.

We have three means of propulsion—a canoe paddle for quiet shore-line fishing; a small pair of oars for the faster water; and a small outboard for the long hauls. The outboard weighs only seventeen pounds but it kicks us along at about eight or ten knots. When not in use, it can be left on the stern or stowed away in the bow as it takes very little space. Now that we have this rig, I can't imagine why we *ever* fooled around with rented boats. The portable boat makes sense, any way you look at it.

Of course, I'm assuming that you keep your reels in reel bags. Also, that you carry an oil can and a screw driver. But how about soap? I have yet to see a satisfactory substitute. Instead of fussing with a small cake of soap, which presents

Incidental Equipment

a carrying problem when wet, we use the soap papers—squares of absorbent paper that have been impregnated with soap. Much handier than a cake of soap.

Last but not least, don't forget that "emergency" pack of cigarettes and some waterproof matches.

CHAPTER 9

Fishing with the Casting Rod

‚ïÑ

EVERY ONCE in a while I pick up an outdoor magazine or a book on angling and find in it a recital of the simplicity and ease with which any intelligent person can master the knack of fishing with a fly rod or a casting rod. Casting is easy, they tell you; nothing to it. A little practice, and you're an expert. This is all you have to do. Then they go on with horse-and-buggy explanations of fundamentals.

It makes just about as much sense to say that golf or trap-shooting or skeet shooting or ski jumping is easy. Sure, a man can take a driver, swing at a golf ball and knock it, maybe, a hundred yards or so. That doesn't make him a golfer. By the same token, anybody who is not a complete moron can take a casting outfit, with one of the antibacklash reels, and heave out a plug for sixty or seventy feet. Does that make him a plug caster? Not by a long shot.

I suppose I have been using a plug rod, off and on, for thirty years. While I lived in Florida, my casting outfit was as much a part of my regular automobile equipment as a jack or a spare tire. On the deck under the rearview window it and a supply of spare plugs went right along with the car. We fished all the time, winter and summer, always with a casting rod. Not only that, but I cast in the N.A.A.C.C. (Na-

Fishing with the Casting Rod

tional Association of Angling and Casting Clubs, formerly N.A.C.A.C.) winter tournament at Orlando, Florida, for two years and managed to walk off with a couple of second-place prizes against such competition as Curly Moulton, Walter Wilman, Walter Frazier, Lou Hurst, Fred Brown, and a lot of other good casters. Yet I don't consider myself a top-flight bait caster by any means. Make up your mind to it—finished performance with a casting rod is not easy.

I'm not saying this to discourage anybody. There is no reason why you can't be a top-notch caster if you really want to be one. But, believe me, you are not going to do it overnight. Good casting requires two things—complete mastery of the fundamentals and a tremendous amount of practice.

Manual dexterity is not necessarily a gift that has been bestowed by a discriminating Providence upon the favored few. To be sure, some men possess it more than others, but it can be developed. All it takes is practice, and more practice, and then some more. How good a caster you wish to become is entirely dependent upon your willingness to study and master the essential *correct* fundamentals, under the guidance, preferably, of a good teacher, and, finally, upon how much time you are willing to devote to the training of your casting hand.

The trouble with most folks is that they will not practice. That is true of fishing or shooting or golf or what have you. Take, for instance, the average hunter. Once or twice a year he takes his shotgun (which probably doesn't fit him) out of its case and goes out after upland game. Naturally, he misses more birds than he hits. Just the same, he comes home all discouraged. Can't hit the side of a barn, he tells the little woman. Then he puts his gun away until the next time. It never occurs to him that if he wants to bring home game he'd better go out to the skeet range and *learn* how to hit birds.

The same thing holds good for fishermen. Nine hundred and ninety-nine of them out of every thousand get their casting practice while they are actually fishing. Not only do they curtail their own sport; during the early stages of backlashes they make things pretty dreary for their boat companions. That sort of business isn't fair to either of them.

Unlike most forms of outdoor sport, you need very little preparation or equipment to practice with your casting rod. All that is required is a tournament plug or casting weight and a strip of lawn. You can leave your casting rig set up and ready for use. Hang it on the wall, where you can have it handy, and use that ten or fifteen minutes before dinner, casting at a target. You will be surprised how soon you will change from merely hitting the target once in a while to hitting it almost every time. Then, when you go out fishing, you need no longer worry about backlashes, you can place your lure exactly where you want it, and you and your companion will have a far more enjoyable day.

When you are practicing casting, don't cast with the side-arm swing that is still all too common among today's bait casters. Before you do anything else, learn the overhead cast, with the rod moving in the vertical plane. Don't be a "side-wheeler." In Texas, they call them "sidewinders" after the little rattlesnakes by that name. Under either name, that sort of a caster is bad news. In the same boat with you, a side-wheeler is actually dangerous. A bass plug, armed with its multiple hooks, can be an exceedingly damaging weapon. There simply isn't room in a boat for that sort of nonsense. That is the reason that I emphasized learning the *correct* fundamentals when you learn bait casting. Not only that— the only way to cast accurately is with the overhead cast, and there is little use in learning to cast at all unless you learn to cast accurately.

Where accuracy pays off, of course, is in shore-line fishing. There every cast is an accuracy cast, aimed at a definite target; at least, it should be. If you can hit that target *every time*, you give yourself a chance to have a good day's fishing.

Fishing with the Casting Rod

If you can merely place your lure in the general vicinity of where it should go, you probably will waste a good deal of your fishing day scaring fish instead of catching them and, worse yet, getting your lure hung up on snags. That, of course, means going in to free it and spoiling a considerable stretch of shore line in the process.

During the years from 1925 to 1927, when we lived in Florida, I met up with a fishing buddy by the name of Jim Barr. Jim lived in Clermont—Clermont in the Hills, they called it. Those hills were all of seventy-five feet high. Maybe even that's an exaggeration, but at least the country wasn't dead flat and that was a welcome relief. Jim was a carpenter. I never was able to make up my mind whether carpentry was a vocation with Jim or merely an avocation—a remunerative but unpleasant side line. In any event, regardless of its economic status, fishing was Jim's first love.

When business took me to Clermont, which was fortunately frequently, I made it a point to consult the weather reports in advance. If the day promised to be fair, I started early, completed my business with the greatest possible dispatch, and then hunted up Jim.

Generally I'd find him on the job, sawing boards or banging away with his hammer. After the first disastrous failure to lure Jim off the job, I learned how to go about things. That first time I made the mistake of suggesting, right out, that Jim knock off work and go fishing.

"Nope," said Jim. "Got to work."

And that was that.

After that I'd go about things differently. The first job was to get Jim away from his tools. He liked to roll his own from brown paper and Bull Durham, so, after the first greeting, I'd sit down on a saw horse or a stack of shingles and break out "the makin's." Once my cigarette was in the poured-out stage, still unrolled, I'd hold out the papers and tobacco in my free hand. That never failed. Jim would stop what he was doing, roll a cigarette, and peace and quiet would reign for the moment.

Jim would lead the way, conversationally. In response to query, I'd tell him whom I had to see in Clermont and approximately why. That was news for Jim to report at home that evening. Then I'd comment on the fact that I'd finished work much earlier than expected. Drive clear over to Clermont, work fifteen minutes, then drive clear back to Orlando. Waste the whole damn day. Too bad. Nice day, too. Jim would nod his head in agreement.

The next move was to talk about tackle.

"Got a new line yesterday," I'd venture.

"That so? What kind?"

"Kingfisher, twelve pound. Picked up an extra spool, just in case."

Before long Jim would be helping me spool that new line on my reel, incidentally pocketing the extra spool with the appropriately polite show of reluctance. This would be followed by casual talk of fishing and another cigarette.

After a half hour or so of this circumlocution, I'd bring things to a focus.

"Well," I'd say, rising, "got to be gettin' on the road. Long drive. Wish it was Saturday so's you could get away. Shame to waste a nice day like this."

At that point Jim would look at the sky and test the breeze with a moist finger.

"Yep; does seem too bad. S'pose your missus would mind if you git home late? I *could* let this job go for one day, anyway."

I would have already told "my missus" not to expect me before midnight, but I'd assure Jim that I'd take a chance.

"Throw yer hat in the door first when you get home," he advised me. "If it stays in, you'll be all right." That was standard comment.

The fact that I had fishing clothes, a bundle of sandwiches

Joe Brooks with a brackish-water Largemouth who fancied a
yellow bass bug.

Frank Bauder with a freshly caught Smallmouth, taken from the Terrytown Level of the North Branch on Joe Messinger's Hair Frog.

Fishing with the Casting Rod

and a thermos of coffee in my car never surprised him. He knew they were there all the time.

Jim had a little square-ended boat that he'd built and a trailer that he'd rigged from the front axle of a Ford. We'd strap this to the rear of my car and set sail. He knew the country and the woods roads and he took me to fishing that not many folks ever see. Not only that, but he knew the hangout of every big bass in the whole area.

Jim refused to take his tackle when we went fishing. He'd never learned the overhead cast, for some reason. Said he'd tried to learn it and finally gave it up. But if he had a man in the front of his boat who knew how to cast, he was perfectly happy to paddle him along the shore lines from dawn till dark. When things were going right, he'd sit back there with his stubby paddle and sing in high falsetto a song about having a gal and her name was Lucy. I certainly learned to know Lucy intimately in a day's fishing with Jim—over and over he'd sing his little song. "I had a gal an' her name was Lucy."

Jim was, I believe, the most finished boatman I know and I have fished with a lot of good ones. He knew that shore-line fishing is a teamwork proposition. He'd spot the boat just right for a cast. Then, while the plug was being fished and retrieved, he'd put the boat in exactly the right location for the next cast. It was up to me to place that plug where Jim wanted it to go. Just let me miss one of Jim's spots or, even worse, spoil one with a bad cast, and the song would stop abruptly. The smooth motion of the boat would change slightly and I'd find myself spotted, with the boat stopped, in the proper location for the next cast. He wouldn't say anything but he surely would let you know if you weren't fishing to suit him. He was an exacting taskmaster, but his critical eye kept me alert and fully on the job, no matter whether the fish were active or not. Naturally, we made a pretty deadly combination.

Black Bass

As I say, Jim had most of the big bass located and when we'd reach one of these places he would tell me about it. Not only that, but he would point out the exact spot, down to a matter of inches, where the plug should land. Believe me, no caster in the National Tournament ever aimed his cast more carefully than I did when I was fishing one of Jim's hot spots. Sometimes we would get the fish and more often we wouldn't, big bass being what they are, but if I fished the place according to Jim's ideas that was all that counted. Then we'd hear some more about Lucy until something else happened.

I learned a lot from Jim, important things that some folks never learn. I found that it pays big dividends to fish a shore line slowly—the slower the better. I found that a difference of as little as six inches or a foot in the placing of some casts is the margin that decides whether or not you get the fish to strike. Jim taught me that stereotyped, cut-to-pattern handling of a plug is no good. He felt that each likely-looking spot presented a separate problem and should be treated according to its individual merits. When fishing with Jim, it wasn't enough merely to make a plug move; it should be made to come alive. Jim is right about that. Individual treatment certainly seems to bring in more fish.

I haven't seen Jim since 1927. If, by fortunate chance, he should see this, I hope that he'll sit himself down and answer some of the letters I wrote him. I'd like nothing better than to go fishing with him again, always assuming that I could manage to pry him loose from his job.

Shore-line fishing, particularly for Largemouth, is a fascinating and exacting pastime. I don't know of any more pleasant way to spend a summer day than to fish the shore line of a good bass lake with a surface lure. There are some tricks to shore-line fishing that it is well to know. For example, it is wise to pay rather special attention to the "points." A point, to make matters clear, is any part of a shore line that

Fishing with the Casting Rod

projects into the lake so that it stands out from its immediate surroundings. Points must be favored feeding spots, as they nearly always mark the homes of large bass. I try to cast slightly beyond a point as the boat approaches it. Then the plug can be worked back gradually, right through the personal territory of Mr. Bass. He may not be hungry but he won't like having his private property invaded, and often he takes steps to repel boarders.

Not all the bass in a lake live along the shore lines, but a great many of them do. When a bass takes up his summer home near a snag or a stump or a pile of slashing, that spot is his and his alone and he will defend it against all comers. Thus, when you cast your plug into his particular bailiwick, you have a double string to your bow. He may hit it because he's hungry and it looks like an easy meal or he may resent the intrusion and take a whack at the seemingly helpless creature out of pure cussedness.

It is always a good plan to place your plug within inches of the probable home of a bass. Suppose, for instance, you are casting to a stump. If your plug lands right next to the stump, you have a good deal more chance of getting a strike than if it lands two or three feet away from it. And if your plug lands wide of the mark, say from six to ten feet, about all you have accomplished with that cast is to let the bass know that something is wrong. You'd better fish out that cast and retrieve your plug rather quickly, as you are probably just wasting time.

Never be in a hurry to play your plug out of a likely-looking spot. A plug that rests motionless on the water is working for you every minute it is there, *providing* that it has been placed in the right location. It is not at all uncommon for bass to knock the daylights out of a plug that has been resting quietly on the water for several minutes while a backlash is being cleared. Fishing is a leisurely business; at least it should be. No doubt about it, haste makes a great deal of waste in fishing, particularly when you are fishing a good shore line.

When you find a down log or a tree toppled into the water, don't cast from a position at right angles to it. Move your boat so that your retrieve will be parallel to the log. That way, fishing it slow, you can fish the whole length of the log with one cast.

Always treat your bass with respect for their natural caution. A bass isn't intelligent—no fish is. If a fish had one grain of sense, we would catch very, very few of them with the methods we use now. Also, a bass isn't scary, in the sense that a trout is. He is a natural scrapper, born with a surly disposition and a chip on his shoulder, and he enjoys a fight. But he has a well-developed sense of caution. If he can see you or if he gets the idea that something is wrong and not as it should be, your chances of getting him are greatly reduced. Thus, it is wise to keep your distance. If you can see objects —branches, stumps, snags, weeds, what have you—under the surface of the water, depend upon it that a bass beside or under one of those objects can see you. That means that you are crowding him—fishing too close. Better move out a bit farther and cut down your handicap.

Another thing—don't make any noise. Sound or vibration travels fast under water just as it does in the air. The bump of a paddle against the boat, the scrape of your feet as you change position, the sound of opening your bait box—any of these and kindred noises will often rob you of a good fish. Talking is just about as bad. The sound of your voice can be heard under water just as it can in the air. To be sure, water cuts down the volume, but fish are extremely sensitive to vibrations and can pick up sounds that we can't hear. If you must talk, keep it down to low tones or whispers.

Izaak Walton gave some sound advice to his pupils. "In times of copious downpour," he said, "seek ye the inlets." That makes sense. An inlet is a natural feeding spot for fish

Fishing with the Casting Rod

and it makes a good place for them to hang around, anyway. An inlet means a fresh supply of cool water, usually well aerated. Naturally it attracts fish. After a hard rain, the inlet will be swollen, and as a rule, muddy. Its turbulent waters carry with them a certain amount of food such as worms, minnows, and luckless insects. The fish know this and gather around for the feast.

When you are fishing an inlet after a rain, remember that the fish are there to feed on what the rushing water brings them. It is a good plan to make your lure behave like some small creature that has fallen into these troubled waters and that is trying to make its way back to shore. Instead of spotting your boat offshore and casting up into the muddy flow, move it to one side so that the retrieve comes out of the muddy water in the general direction of shore. Usually you will get most of your strikes right at the borderline, where muddy water and clear water meet.

Again, you can use exactly the opposite technique. Shoreline minnows and small fish such as shiners, perch, rock bass, etc., are just as interested in finding food in that muddy water as are the bass. Also, a small fish, when he finds himself in danger, will welcome the cloudy shelter of muddy water. With this in mind, it is often productive to cast across a muddy flow into the clear water beyond it, retrieving your lure toward the cloudy water instead of away from it.

One day in the East Branch of the Delaware River I employed this method with excellent success. There had been a sharp thunder shower that lasted for only about fifteen or twenty minutes—not enough to discolor the main river but enough to make muddy torrents of every little feeder stream. One of these poured into the head of a long flat pool, leaving a well-defined yellow streak along one shore line. Beginning at the upper end of the pool, I waded down along the shore, making my way slowly in the muddy water and casting a streamer out into the clear water. I don't recall ever having had a busier day on the Delaware. The cast and retrieve that did not produce a strike was very much the exception.

There are several types of shore lines and they require different treatment. Consider first the typical marsh shore line such as you will encounter so often in Florida. There the shore line consists merely of reedy marsh growth, which drops off suddenly into deep water. You can handle such a shore line in two different ways—fish it with a surface or popping lure, or use a deep-running underwater lure.

Lake Helenblazes, Florida, had that sort of a shore line. My goodness! What a place *that* was to fish! It's all changed now, they tell me. The channel of the river has been cut out and opened to boat traffic and you can crank up the outboard and sail right upriver through Lake Washington, Sawgrass Lake, the North Channel, and into "Blazes." On the more recent maps they've even changed the name, but on the old maps it stands, plain for all to read, "Lake Helenblazes."

Time was, back in 1925 and 1926, when going into Blazes—the lost lake—was no mean undertaking. There being no choice in the matter, we made the journey in one day. We would leave Orlando at about two A.M. and drive the seventy-odd miles to Bob Wall's camp at the intersection of the St. Johns River and the Melbourne-Kissimmee Highway. With any luck, we would reach Bob's camp just at daybreak. Bob would have the boats ready, with motors in place and gas cans full. We would transfer our gear from car to boats and get under way. Bob would go upriver several miles and then turn into the main drainage canal. We would go to the end of the excavation and then strike off due north through the marsh. This last part of the journey had to be done with long push poles as a means of propulsion. We figured we had made good time if we reached Blazes by ten o'clock.

This lake, as you probably know, is the source of the St. Johns River. Beginning, probably, as an alligator hole it has been scoured out of the marsh proper by years of erosion by

Fishing with the Casting Rod

wind-driven "floating islands"—large sections of floating marsh growth that have broken loose from the marsh proper. These floating masses of intermeshed vegetation are big and heavy and they have done a good job of lake building; Blazes is quite large and surprisingly deep. The water is brown, but it is cool (for Florida) and quite clear. Evidently the discoloration by vegetable growth is to the liking of the bass because they surely were there in quantity.

When we fished it, it was a simple matter to boat two hundred bass in a day's fishing. We didn't keep many—never anything under five pounds—and we brought out only the big ones. The first time I fished it our two boats brought back to camp nine bass that weighed a total of seventy-eight pounds.

We fished it entirely with surface lures. At times I think we might have done better with deep-running lures, but all of us liked to see those big sod-busters lay into a floating plug. I saw seven bass one day, all taken in Blazes, that really made my eyes pop. They lay in the bottom of a boat, covered with a wet burlap bag or two to keep them fresh. The big one was just under fifteen pounds and the little one topped eight pounds by a few ounces. These had been taken off the bottom with an Al Foss Shimmy Wiggler and a pork rind. However, we were content to stick to a surface lure.

There wasn't much variety to the Blazes shore line. Mostly it was simply marsh edge, sliced off straight, with few indentations or coves. The system was to cast right in close, as close as you could get it, to the edge of the marsh. Then it was up to you to keep your plug alive and still not move it away from the marsh edge. The bass lived mostly under the sawed-off edge, and a plug that was five or six feet out had lost much of its usefulness. Naturally, we chose plugs that would kick up quite a bit of fuss without much forward motion. Heddon's "Lucky 13" was one of these. Its long lower lip would tend to slant the drift of the plug away from you after you had twitched the rod tip to make the plug move. I still have the old "Lucky 13" that accounted for my largest bass—fourteen pounds, four ounces—and the poor old thing certainly looks as though it had been to the wars. And come to think of it, it has.

Another favorite was Creek Chub's Injured Minnow, or as we called it, "the crip" or "the crippled minnow." This one has little action of its own, but it has small propellers fore and aft and the slightest motion causes these to whirl. You can get a surprising amount of activity out of that plug with very little forward motion.

As soon as the plug had played itself several feet away from the marsh, we would retrieve rapidly, not fishing, and recast. Of course, the hot spots, such as coves, points, side channels, and so on, received extra-special care as usually these places had been pre-empted by big fish, but mostly it was simply a case of casting to the marsh edge.

With the deep-running plug, the casting technique is about the same; cast to the marsh edge, as close as you can get it. Then let the lure sink, right straight down to the bottom, before you start the slow, irregular retrieve. It isn't nearly as much fun as surface fishing but it does catch bass.

As I say, the channel to Blazes is all open now and the cream has been skimmed off that magnificent fishing. I'm thankful that I was lucky enough to fish Blazes while it was still difficult of access. There is no better way to spoil good fishing than to make it easy to reach.

Another type of shore line that requires somewhat different treatment is the one that drops off into shallow water. Flowage areas usually have this sort of shoreline. Here, of course, deep-running lures are of little use. For this fishing we use a compromise—the plug that can be fished either as a surface lure or a shallow-running lure with plenty of action. Good examples of this type are the Bass-Oreno plugs, the Flatfish, or the Creek Chub "Two Thousand." These can be played very

Fishing with the Casting Rod

well as surface lures. Then, when retrieved, they are working for you right back to the boat.

Usually a shore line of this type is overhung with foliage such as trees and bushes. It is here that any practice casting you may have done really pays off. An overhung shore line presents all manner of casting problems. You should be able to bullet your lure in under low-hanging branches with a flat-trajectory cast that will get it back in there where it belongs. Again, you should be able to throw a high, looping cast that will clear intervening obstacles and let you fish the back-behind nooks, crannies, and pot holes that the average fisherman doesn't reach. While a weedless spoon or wobbler is a safer lure to use for this sort of fishing, it is possible, if you are as accurate as you should be, to use a regulation plug. If you are fairly sure of hitting your target, you can cast to the far side of a pot hole, fish it out, and then jump your plug out of danger with a quick lift of the rod tip against a tight line.

When flowage lands are cleared, before flooding, it seems to be the accepted method to remove all usable timber and allow the slashing to lie where it falls. Of course, a lot of this debris floats away when the land is flooded, but a lot of it does not. Then comes the gradual process of decay which eventually transforms this waterlogged wood into silt. Bass seem to enjoy living in this cluttered-up hodgepodge of stumps and tangled branches. Fishing a newly made flowage is often pretty much of a headache.

Of course, in difficult territory such as this, long casts are impractical. Thus, it is your job to out-guess the bass. If the top of a stump is submerged, always cast over the top of it and play your lure on the surface at the far side. The same holds good for brush piles, down logs, and such. Of course, if you hook a fish, you must take the boat to him instead of trying to bring him to the boat.

Mystery Pond, Vermont, which I mentioned earlier, is just

such a place. This is an artificial lake, made by damming up
the Clyde River. The old channel is quite deep but the rest
of Mystery Pond is shallow and incumbered with the leftovers from lumbering operations. It has all types of shore line,
but by far the best fishing is on the flats, among the stumps
and half-submerged brush piles. I would rather raise a bass
along an open-water shore line, but we get so much better
fishing on the shallow flats that there is where we spend most
of our time.

When you fish the weed beds and the lily pads, you had
best put away the plugs and use metal lures. Of course, there
are weedless plugs, but even the best of them don't perform
in the weeds in comparison with the spoons, spinners, and
wobblers. If you happen to be a pork-chunk fan, that, too, is
an excellent lure for weedy places, particularly if the water
is not too deep. In deep water, however, you want your lure
near the bottom, and the fast-sinking metal lures will fish
right down deep among the weeds if you want them to. As
a matter of fact, the heavy wobblers are the only lures that
I can find that *will* fish deep among heavy weeds. These, of
course, should be dressed up with a rubber "hula skirt" or a
piece of pork rind. This trimming does not lessen their efficiency and it adds greatly to their fish-taking ability.

Fishing the weeds brings up another kindred topic—"dry-
line" bait casting. Up to now, there seems to be no clearly
defined notion as to the exact nature of dry-line casting.
Some maintain that a pork chunk, unweighted and with
merely a weedless hook, when cast among the weeds, rushes,
and lily pads, climbs its way back to you over, around, and
through the weeds, enabling you to keep a tight line that can
be held free of the water and giving you theoretically perfect
dry-line fishing. Others say that dry-line casting means the
treatment of the line with dressing so that it becomes waterproof and floats "dry," as a dry fly floats. I'm not sure which
definition is correct. Unquestionably a dressed line will per-

mit slower and easier fishing of a surface lure, but I'm not convinced that it is worth the time and trouble.

In 1945, three of us journeyed to Georgian Bay, Ontario, to do some bass fishing. We arrived there in late July and found that the temperature setup of the lake—the thermocline—had become quite well established. The countless islands sheltered the fishing areas so thoroughly that the wind had no opportunity to turn over the temperature layers, with the result that the Smallmouth were down at about the twenty-foot level. You could fill a boat with them if you cared to use bait, but after one session of that we sought other fields of activity.

Our guide took us to several bays, some of them completely choked with rushes and lily pads, both large and small, and there we fished for Largemouth. For about ten days we had a circus with those bass. Never anywhere have I seen such beautifully conditioned Largemouth. Black as your hat on top, they shaded off to light silver and cream, and they were deep, fat, husky battlers, every one of them.

After a few tries, we gave up plugs in favor of deep-running wobblers with the usual trimmings. However, the weeds were so thick that it was almost impossible to land a heavy bass in them. Nine times out of ten he would wind up the line in the weeds and bust things all to hell before you could get the boat anywhere near him. The mortality rate among metal lures was inordinately high, but we had plenty of excitement and a lot of fun.

As I said earlier, not all of the bass in a lake live along shore. A great many of them live in the open water. This is particularly true of Smallmouth. Around the bars and shoals offshore they can find exactly the temperatures they prefer and enough food to keep them well fed and happy. Unlike the shore-line residents, who prefer to live alone, the open-water bass are quite gregarious and stay pretty much in schools.

Learning open-water fishing and locating the feeding areas

and concentration spots is a study of itself. The good fishing spots around the bars and shoals are every bit as well defined as the hot spots along the shore lines. A difference of as little as ten or twenty feet in the location of your boat often spells the difference between good fishing or no fishing at all. You can't be too careful when you mark the exact location of an open-water concentration area.

Learning the fishing spots in a lake is easier, of course, if you have a competent guide who is familiar with the bars and shoals. However, you can do it by yourself. There are two methods—trolling and drifting with the wind.

Before attempting to find out anything about a new lake, it is a good idea to get a map of the lake so that you can do the job systematically. A topographic map of the area will give you the shape of the lake and the compass points. With this, you can easily draw your own map and set in the land marks on shore as guides. Be sure to draw your working map large enough to permit marking locations on it and making notes.

If you use the trolling method (and there is no more deadly tiresome way of fishing), chart each course and row across and back, from one landmark to another. Best use a deep-running lure so that you can get right down there where the fish live. Indicate each course on your map so that there will be no duplication of effort in your survey. When you get a strike or hook a fish, take cross bearings on shore immediately. Then troll back through that area several times to make sure you know where the probable concentration spot lies.

As I say, open-water bass usually hang around together in schools, and where you find one fish there are usually more. The job is to find the exact location of their stamping grounds. This done, take your bearings on shore and then note them carefully beside the spot you have marked on your map.

There are two ways to take cross bearings. One is to draw an imaginary line between landmarks on opposite shores, say

Fishing with the Casting Rod

to the north and south. Then draw another imaginary line between two more landmarks to the east and west. The other way, and the more accurate one, is to drop your anchor, so that your boat won't change position while you take bearings. Then look around and find two obvious bearings on the same shore, one behind the other. For instance, a tall pine at the water's edge may be in line with a red barn directly behind it but half a mile away on a hill. Make a notation on your map like this—"S.W.—tall pine—red barn." Then, approximately at right angles to the first bearing, find two more landmarks that are in line, say a big white rock on shore and a fence corner in a distant field. Set this down too, "N.W.—big white rock, shore—fence corner, corn field." With this method you can get cross bearings that will mark a good fishing spot for you down to a few feet.

If you are doing your prospecting by yourself, drifting with the wind is easier than trolling. The thing to do first is to row to the upwind end of the lake. With this method, an outboard motor is a big help. Once at the upwind end, start your drift by placing your boat opposite a prominent landmark. Then let the wind blow you downlake and cast as you go, first one side then the other. When you hook a fish, land him as soon as you can, row back to the approximate spot where you hooked him, and drop anchor. Then comb the area thoroughly with a deep-running lure. If you find more bass, set down the location on your map for future reference.

Pay particular attention to bars and shoals. Learn, if you can, their general comformation, as this knowledge will be useful when you are fishing them. When fishing a shoal, instead of casting up to it from deep water, I like to anchor my boat right on the shoal. Then the trick is to cast well out into deep water, let the lure sink down close to the bottom, and then retrieve, slowly and erratically, up the slope of the shoal. That way, the lure can be made to follow the conformation of the bottom and it is more productive.

But to get back to drifting with the wind—one drift, from the upwind shore to the downwind shore, will cover a strip about two hundred feet wide. All right, crank up the motor and go back to the upwind shore again. Then spot your boat so that your next drift will parallel the first one with the two strips not quite overlapping. Mark each drift on the back of your map or in a notebook. It will take you a while to cover a lake thoroughly, but when you finish you will have learned quite a lot about that body of water.

In open-water fishing, accuracy doesn't enter the picture. Largely it's a matter of heave and hope. It isn't as much fun as shore-line fishing but when the bass are in deep water, and this is particularly true of Smallmouth, it certainly is the way to fish for them.

When a lake is broken up by islands as is the Georgian Bay area of Lake Ontario, get your guide to show you the passes or "thoroughfares" between the islands. There is nearly always a current in these places and the fish concentrate in the backwaters beside these currents to pick up what food may drift by. Here, too, a deep-running lure is the order of the day as the fish usually lie deep and will not come up for a shallow-running lure. Use a plug or a wobbler that will retrieve easily at depths of twenty feet or more and you will usually get more strikes.

Of course, there is always a great deal of discussion and difference of opinion among anglers as to the size of the plug that is most effective. It is pretty hard to lay down hard and fast rules on this subject but there are some generalities on the matter of size that seem to hold good, year after year.

First off, I'm assuming that you like to fish for big bass. In general, big Smallmouth seem to prefer the midget plugs while a big Largemouth likes a good, big mouthful. Let's take a look at some concrete examples of this preference.

Fishing with the Casting Rod

About sixty-five miles from the desk where this is being set down is the North Branch of the Susquehanna River. This stream holds a truly astonishing supply of big Smallmouth, and by "big," I mean bass that will go from three to five pounds. As a matter of fact, a three pounder doesn't excite very much comment. Naturally, these fish have seen a great many plugs. I have tossed five-eighth-ounce Jitterbugs and Flatfish and what-have-you over them for hours on end with even less than indifferent results. Actually, the only success-ful plug fishermen on that stream are the men who fish after dark. At night the big boys will take a whack at a five-eighth-ounce surface lure now and then, but in the daytime a five-eighth-ounce lure, either surface or underwater, is definitely not productive.

About four years ago, Erney Hille and I invaded the North Branch with light-lure outfits and midget plugs—little fellows, quarter- and three-eighth-ounce. The first time we tried this we used light nylon leaders and four-pound lines. In one afternoon we hooked more big bass than the average bait fisherman will see in a month of serious fishing. We learned, to our regret, that there is entirely too much potential trouble in that river to attempt to handle big bass on four-pound lines. In all, we lost eight plugs and leaders by having those old busters duck behind boulders, under ledges, around snags, and bust the hell out of things. Now we use seven-and-a-half-pound nylon lines (which really test out at about nine pounds) and we can put some pressure on these big fish and lead them out into deep water, away from trouble. But the important thing is that we can hook these big bass on midget plugs whereas we couldn't interest them in the larger plugs—and by that, I mean we can take them consistently. The same thing holds true down at Conowingo Dam, in the lower Susquehanna, a few miles above tidewater.

A Largemouth, as you very well know, responds to practically any sort of a plug if he happens to be in a striking

Black Bass

mood. But big Largemouth are choosy. If you want big ones consistently, you must give them what they like.

Now and then one of the big boys will fall for one of the little plugs, the three-eighth-ounce or smaller. By the same token, a big one will absorb a small bass bug once in a while. But by and large, day in and day out, a big Largemouth likes a big lure.

We hit on the idea of big plugs for big Largemouth more or less accidentally one day in Maine. Dick was a little fellow then, twelve years old, and he was just learning to use a bait-casting outfit. It was in July and the trout were down deep. We could pick up a few now and then in the evenings, but the daytime fishing was pretty dull. Seeking something to keep us occupied during the day, we asked our host if there was any bass fishing in the neighborhood. He allowed as how there was, but, with the true down-Easter's disdain for "them mud cats," declined to have anything to do with such nonsense. Only under pressure did he give us directions for reaching Forbes Pond, and he cautioned us not to bring any bass home with us as "they wan't fit to eat."

We found Forbes Pond all right and paid the farmer fifty cents for boat rental. That boat was something—big, incredibly heavy, and in need of paint and caulking. One of the oars was cracked and it had been repaired with a wrapping of hay wire. As there was a strong wind blowing, it was out of the question to expect Dick to row, so I located him on the stern seat with the plug rod and we set sail. After considerable effort I managed to get the boat in position near a likely-looking shore line and I told Dick to get to work. He was using an orthodox five-eighth-ounce plug, I've forgotten what kind, and his first cast—downwind, mind you—produced a bird's nest in his reel that seemed impossible. Nothing for it but to break my back holding that heavy scow up into the wind while he picked out loops of line. At last he was clear

Fishing with the Casting Rod

and he cast again. This time the plug went out and was taken at once by a small bass.

In all the years and the many places I have fished, I don't remember any waters, anywhere, that held more fish. It didn't make any difference where Dick put that plug. All he had to do was to get it away from the boat. Sometimes two or three fish fought for it and if he lost a fish, more often than not he would hook another on the same retrieve. The trouble was that Dick managed to get the plug away from the boat only once in a while. The rest of the time was spent in picking out backlashes.

At last, in desperation, I pulled the Robert E. Lee into a cove and beached her. Then I went through the tackle box. What I wanted was something big enough and heavy enough to take line away from that reel as fast as the thing would roll it out.

After looking over the supply, I selected a creation called Heddon's Game Fisher. This was sold to me in Toronto as a musky plug. It had two swivel joints through its midriff, a beak like a duckbilled platypus, and its paint job was, and still is, yellow with pink trim. I had never cast this plug and I knew nothing about its behavior. However, it was big and heavy and that was what I wanted. You may recall that I spoke of this plug earlier when talking about the underfed bass of Derby Pond, Vermont.

Dick wound up and heaved this doubtful affair out with the wind and, praise be, it sailed away without complication. Then, for the first time, I had a chance to see it in action. In the boat it looked awful, but in action it had a wiggle that would make any hula dancer envious. Promptly we christened it Mae West.

Mae hadn't minced her way through the reeds more than about four feet when an old buster of a bass came from nowhere and knocked her endways. The explosive strike and the size of the rumpus took Dick off guard. The reel handle

Black Bass

flew out of his hand and a truly monumental bird's nest built up and overflowed from the reel before Dick gathered his wits. Eventually this was cleared and order restored. The fish, of course, had gone about his business.

In due course, Dick managed to cast this big plug fairly well. Then I began to realize that, while we weren't raising as many fish as we had with a smaller lure, the ones we did raise were large fish. Dick's inexpert hands weren't equal to the task of handling these old busters and we landed only a few of them. But, believe me, we had plenty of excitement.

Since then both Dick and I have cast Mae West in many bass waters. She is scratched and beaten and battle scarred. But of all our lures, we have taken more big Largemouth who fell for her insidious behavior than we have on any two of our other models, and we have fished it in the Middle West, Ontario, and along the Atlantic seaboard from Maine to the Carolinas.

When all is said and done, bait casting can be just about what you want to make it. If you are content to cast indifferently and reel in your lure rather lackadaisically, bait casting can be a pretty stupid and tiresome piece of business. However, if you are willing to practice your casting, sharpening up your accuracy and your general technique, and eliminating backlashes, you can have a lot of fun with a casting outfit and, incidentally, produce a lot of fish.

At most any bookshop or sporting-goods store you can find books on casting. No need here to go into detail. For that matter, there isn't much detail to go into. You know that you should hold the rod with the reel handles on top, not at the side. Aim your cast, holding the rod at about thirty degrees above the horizontal. Then back fast, in the vertical plane, stopping at about "one o'clock." Then forward *twice* as fast, releasing thumb pressure on the spool just before you complete the forward motion. Don't take your thumb completely off the spool. Merely ease up on the pressure and maintain

Fishing with the Casting Rod

light contact as the spool turns. Try to make your casting motion consist almost entirely of wrist action, moving the forearm as little as possible and the upper arm not at all. If you will watch a good professional, you will absorb the whole idea in five minutes. Then, once you have the fundamentals and know what you should do, all you need is practice. Believe me, it pays off in added fishing pleasure.

CHAPTER 10

Fishing with the Fly Rod

CONTRARY TO RATHER common belief, fly-rod fishing for bass is not new. President Grover Cleveland, who spent his declining years at Princeton, New Jersey, used to have himself a time fly fishing for bass. So did Dr. J. A. Henshall, back around 1880. However, this sport was practiced at that time only by a few men. Bait fishing was the way to take bass. Flies were for trout.

For some reason, fly fishing for bass has lacked popular appeal and has failed to keep pace with the improvement in tackle and methods that has been evidenced in trout fishing. Today most any tackle store can supply you with up-to-date trout tackle, but try to find good fly-rod equipment for bass fishing! I tell you, it's a job. The rods are stiff, fast-action affairs that will wreck your casting hand in half an hour. The reels, with a few outstanding exceptions, are badly designed and short lived. Most terminal tackle—streamers and bass bugs—is not fit to take up room in your kit. Happily, the line companies are turning out good lines, but these, too, can be improved upon. As recently as June, 1948, Joe Brooks, of Baltimore, and I were discussing the bass-fly-rod problem. So far as we know—and I think we know about most of the good models—there isn't a single rod company today that

Fishing with the Fly Rod

puts out a *standardized* model in a bass fly rod that can rightly be called a good rod. The Knight Ninety-Nine is a good rod if you can get one that is tapered according to the original design, but for some reason the company that turns out this rod refuses to standardize the model.

As I say, fly fishing for bass has lagged far behind trout fishing. In witness of this, let me quote from *The Book of the Black Bass* by Dr. J. A. Henshall, published in 1881. This is what he says: "It is useless to cast a fly for black bass on perfectly smooth water."

With the fly-rod tackle that was available in 1880, it is quite understandable how the good doctor could bring himself to make such an astonishing and positive statement. But here's the pay-off—in the *Forest and Stream Sportsmen's Encyclopedia*, published in 1923, about three hundred words were devoted to the instruction of the reader in the science of fly fishing for black bass. This masterful exposition begins with that very quotation from Dr. Henshall's book. As I say, the bass fishermen learn slowly.

My introduction to fly fishing for bass came about, of all places, on our golf course. I was playing one July day with a middle-aged physician who was an ardent follower of all of the outdoor sports. Somehow the talk turned to bass fishing, and he asked me how I fished for them. I told him I used live bait, helgramites mostly. Then came my first instructions in fly fishing for bass.

"You'll have no trouble," he told me, "getting your limit of bass most any day you go out if you'll do what I tell you. Go down to the sporting-goods store and buy the longest cane pole they have in the place. Rig this pole with a heavy line, tying it, good and tight, well down on the pole and then work your way toward the tip, taking a half hitch around the pole about every six inches. Allow about rod length of line to hang from the tip. Say your pole is eighteen or twenty feet long—that will give you about a thirty-six- or a forty-foot cast.

"Tie a heavy three-foot leader to the end of your line and then fasten a regular pickerel spoon to the end of your leader. You know the kind, a fluted Skinner spoon, nickel-plated, with a treble hook trimmed with red and white feathers."

"Take this rig and your fish basket—that's all you'll need—up Lycoming Creek. Cast your spoon out across the tail of a riffle, just where it breaks into the pool, and let the current swing it across and down for you. When you fish out that riffle, go ashore and walk down to the tail of the pool. Wade out quietly and cast across the tail, just above where the flat water breaks into the next riffle. By the time you've fished eight or ten pools that way you ought to have your basket full."

I listened to all of this respectfully but with disbelief. Bass on a pickerel spoon! Silly! The whole idea was so completely at variance with everything I had learned about bass fishing that it didn't make any sense at all. I charged it up to the casual imaginings of a senile mind and forgot about it.

The following year I was fishing Pine Creek one afternoon. The bass were inactive and the fishing was dull. I had taken with me a new rod—a cheap eight-foot affair that was jointed into six or seven pieces. Sunday rods, they were called, because they could be concealed under a coat or packed in a suitcase. Curious to know whether or not this creation actually would cast a fly, I removed the bait hook from my leader and tied on a small spinner-and-fly combination. Then I waded out into the stream far enough to give me a clear backcast and tossed my spinner-and-fly rig out over the tail of the riffle. On about the third or fourth cast my fly was taken with a savage, smashing strike and I was fast to a large and active bass. Automatically, when the fish

Fishing with the Fly Rod

struck I struck back—action and reaction, I suppose. With that the cheap Sunday rod parted at the second ferrule and the two top sections detached themselves from the working rod and slid down the line. Perhaps the bass saw them coming toward him. At all events, he made a determined effort to depart from that vicinity. Down he went through the pool, the cheap reel screaming bloody murder. When I applied extra pressure to stop him, two or three more sections of the rod broke free and slid down the line, leaving me with a short piece of what had been a fly rod, a rod grip, and a reel. Fortunately the heavy line and leader held, and after a long tussle I managed to beach the fish.

A brief survey showed that the rod was beyond repair. The inferior wood had broken cleanly, without splinters, evidently from dry rot. So I sat there on the sloping beach and looked at the bass and the fly that had taken him. Then I remembered the doctor on the golf course and his advice about the use of the pickerel spoon. That was in 1915.

You remember that I told you about my struggles to find a good bass fly rod, finally solving the problem by making one. The next chore was to find some terminal tackle. At first I contented myself with "bass flies" (oversize trout flies) and salmon flies. Then, in desperation, I learned to tie my own flies and in that way managed to get what I wanted.

Knowing nothing of bass bugs, I confined my early fly-rod efforts to spoon and fly. The problem of getting good spoons eventually was solved by having dies made at the local die plant and stamping out my own spoons and saddles.

I don't suppose that I will ever forget my first visit to the Delaware River. I was living in Binghamton, New York, at the time, so I made inquiry and learned that Deposit, New York, was the closest Delaware fishing. I loaded my gear into my car one morning and set sail.

Black Bass

When I got to Deposit I drove to the river and parked my car. Evidently there had been some rain up the valley as the river was somewhat discolored, but there was some visibility so I walked down the bank and into the pool under the old covered bridge. I had never fished the Delaware and knew nothing of the water, so I figured one place was as good as another at which to start operations.

Walking to the tail of the riffle at the head of the pool, I cast my rig out into its troubled waters. Nothing happened, so I walked downstream a few yards and cast again. Then I noticed that I had an audience. Seated on the stone wall that flanked the ramp of the bridge were two old-timers, probably bass fishermen. Sound travels over water and I could hear them talking.

"Hey, Ed," said one. "Look at that durn fool, throwin' that little spoon-hook around the eddy. What'n hell does he think he's gonna ketch?"

".Dunno," replied Ed. "Takes all kind o'people."

Just then I had a heavy strike, immediately followed by a spectacular leap.

"Hey, Ed! Fer Christ's sake! *He's got a bass!*"

No doubt about it—I had indeed "got a bass"—about two pounds of determined, untiring, tough river Smallmouth. I managed to subdue him at last, net him, and put him in my creel. Then I waded back into the pool and recast. Almost immediately I had on another bass, this one even larger than the first.

My critics on the bridge ramp had changed their ideas about "that little spoon-hook" by this time. For a while they shouted words of encouragement and advice. At last, unable to stand the pressure any longer, they climbed down the bank and demanded to see my tackle. Up to my hips in water and a safe distance away, I granted them a brief glimpse of the "spoon-hook" by dangling it from my fingers. Then I went on with my fishing.

Fishing with the Fly Rod

At that time the New York State limit was fifteen bass per day. Conservation was merely a word in the dictionary. In an hour and a half I had removed my limit of lusty bass from that pool and was on my way home. Since then, I can't remember a year when I haven't fished the friendly waters of the Delaware at least once or twice. My son, Dick, has fished it with me since he was eleven years old and we have taken from its sparkling reaches literally thousands of river Smallmouth. We don't keep many of them, merely enough for an occasional meal, but each year we manage to "educate" a right considerable number of Delaware bass.

During recent years, we have seen fly-rod men in the Delaware once in a while. Not often, but we have seen them. Not that many of them do any great execution among the bass of that river, but they are learning. One summer not so long ago I met two young men on the bank of the pool under the bridge at Deposit. They wore sport shirts, bathing trunks, and sneakers and they carried bamboo fly rods.

I greeted them cordially enough and to my surprise, received a rather chilly reception. In response to my inquiry, they said they'd been doing O.K. "We don't bother with bait," one explained. "We're *fly fishing*," this with pronounced emphasis. I acted properly impressed and retired to the seat of an old rowboat to watch what went on.

Preparations complete, they walked into the stream, side by side, and proceeded to wade down the center of the pool, almost armpit deep, casting tiny spoons and what looked like #10 flies ahead of them. These boys were not advocates of the high backcast. Instead, they laid their backcasts out on the water behind them (one actually caught an alert chub on his backcast) and then heaved the forward cast up and over, getting out the fly about forty feet at most. As might be expected, they really made inroads on the rock bass-sun-fish-chub population, now and then raising a small bass.

Black Bass

When I saw how things were going, I walked down the bank and asked if they had any objection to my fishing the far shore line explaining that I would not interfere with their fishing. They said, almost in unison, "Hell, no, go ahead," and paid no more attention to me.

It so happened that there was a Solunar Period in progress and, as I had suspected, the bass were along shore, looking for a meal. On my third cast, a fairly able bass took my bass bug and the war was on.

Before I left for the river that morning, my better half and general manager had given me orders to bring home a mess of fish. Usually she tells me *not* to bring home any, but this time she wanted some bass, so it was up to me to produce. Fishing ahead of me down the shallow shore line, I hooked and landed five nice Delaware bass. The boys in the middle of the pool said nothing and went on with their "fly fishing." At last, down toward the tail of the pool, I hooked my last bass, this one well over two pounds. Then came the one and only comment from midriver.

"Hey, Jim," said one, "let's get out of here. That big bastard just hooked another bass."

Now, here's a rather surprising statement. I've said it before and I'll probably say it many times before I die, but I think it is both true and important. Fly-rod fishing for bass, and particularly bass-bug fishing, is the most difficult form of fresh-water angling. Not that bass are so tough to catch if your equipment is good and your technique is correct. Bass respond quite readily to a well-presented lure. Brown trout, without question, are the toughest of our fresh-water game fish to catch consistently, but casting a trout fly is child's play when compared to casting a bass bug.

As stated before, a bass bug, to be fished efficiently in open water, should be handled with sixty-five or seventy feet of line, if not more. A bass bug, when compared with a trout fly,

Fishing with the Fly Rod

is a heavy lure. It needs a heavy line to carry it out where you want it to go. That, of course, requires a big rod. If you take your time, there should be no difficulty in landing adult bass on light trout tackle. Yet you can't begin to cast a bass bug with that same tackle. It is the casting job, not the size of the fish, that determines the size and design of your tackle.

Long-line casting with any sort of terminal gear, regardless of size, requires correct timing. A bass bug, having comparatively high air resistance and weight, places decided accent on timing. To illustrate, you can commit all manner of casting crimes with a dry fly and still get the fly out where you want it. The same technique with a bass bug would get you exactly no place. As I say, I can count the good bug casters of my acquaintance on the thumb and fingers of one hand, and that goes for both professionals and amateurs.

Of course, you can learn the fundamentals of sound timing from any good book on casting. There is not space here to cover the matter thoroughly. However, I can give you two or three useful hints. Learn to hold your rod correctly, with your thumb on the side and the palm of your hand facing the direction of the cast; learn to throw your backcast high; don't start your forward cast until the bug has *almost* completed its rearward journey. Another thing—don't try to pick up too much line from the water. Depend on the shoot to give you distance, rather than the pickup. A good man can shoot thirty feet of bug line—ten feet on the backcast and the other twenty on the forward cast.

When fishing a lake or a nonwadable river with a bass bug, it is best to cast the bug either slightly ahead of the boat or directly at right angles to its location. The boat should be kept well out when fishing the open-water shore lines and the caster should handle at least sixty-five or seventy feet of line. If we have any choice in the matter, we prefer to paddle the boat rather than to row it. A paddle makes so much

Black Bass

less fuss than oars, regardless of how careful the rower may be. Dick and I being right-handed casters, prefer to fish a lake in a clockwise direction. This places the shore line on the left of the man in the prow, allowing him to manipulate his tackle out over the front of the boat. Moving the other way, so that the bass bug must travel back and forth over the center of the boat is a little dangerous, as a careless cast may cause the bug to hook the paddler. Of course, when it is necessary to row, the caster sits or stands in the stern of the boat. Then the direction of motion must be reversed unless the rower wishes to push the boat along backward. In any event, the matter should be so arranged that the fisherman casts over the end of the boat and not across it.

When we are fishing streamers, spinner-flies, or sinking metal lures, we always allow the motion of the boat to help rather than to hinder the angler. Thus, if the angler wishes to fish deep, getting the lure well under, we move the boat with the current or, in still water, toward the direction of the cast so that the boat's motion will place no tension on the lines. If we want to fish these lures fairly shallow, then the motion of the boat is reversed.

When we are wading, then it is a case of every man for himself. In a wadable river, we vary the direction of our casts so as to take advantage of the current. If we are fishing the shore line of a fairly still pool, we wade deep and cast in at right angles to the shore line. If we are fishing a feeding run, we cast obliquely across and let the current swing the lure across and below. In fast or medium-fast water, a line that is cast at right angles to the current as ofen as not will develop a bow and impede quick striking.

Where the depth of the water in a pool prevents wading out far enough to cast at right angles, then we wade at comfortable depth and cast downstream ahead of us. Bass lures, for the most part, depend upon action to make them effective.

Fishing with the Fly Rod

Thus, except when we are fishing dry flies to a hatch of Mayflies, we always try to take advantage of current action. When fishing the feeding lane or "thread of the stream," for instance, we wade well to one side of it and cast obliquely across and down, letting the current help us fish the area thoroughly from one side to the other. Of course, if we wish to fish sinking lures well down near the bottom, we cast obliquely up and across, allowing line, leader, and lure to sink before starting the retrieve.

While we're at it, let's talk a little about line handling. The rules are somewhat different than in trout fishing. The conventional way to handle excess line—shooting line—is to hold it in coils in the left hand. Well, that's all right if you want to shoot ten or twelve feet. But when you employ twenty or thirty feet of excess line, coils in the left hand nearly always tangle. Even if you hang individual coils over separate fingers, you are bound to get tangles and that is a nuisance. After fooling around with coils for much too long, I gave it up. Now, if I'm fishing from a boat or a canoe, I let the stripped-in line coil itself on the bottom of the boat between my feet. If I'm wading, I let the line hang down into the water. If it is dressed, as it should be, it floats on the surface and the current keeps it out of your way. In shallow water you must be careful not to step on it as that usually means a ruined line. That is about the only hazard.

Aside from tangles, there is another reason for avoiding coils in your left hand. When you first cast your bug, your rod is pointing in its general direction as the bug strikes the the water. *Don't* play the bug by raising the rod tip. Instead, keep your rod down, parallel to the water, and strip in slack line as it accumulates. To do this, lay the line over a finger of your casting hand—either the index finger or the middle finger, depending on personal preference—and use your left hand for stripping in a foot or two at a time. That way, you always have tight line on your bug and your rod stays in striking position. You can't do this nearly as handily if you carry coils in your left hand.

Make it a rule never to be in a hurry when you are fishing a bass bug. With a streamer fly or a metal lure, a certain amount of action is necessary to make it effective, but a bass bug is working for you the moment it touches the water, regardless of motion. I have seen bass take a bug after it has been resting quietly on the surface for a full minute or more. Believe me, haste makes waste with a bass bug. Bug fishing is a leisurely business and the slower you can do it, the better will be the results. In a river, the current often allows you little choice but to fish faster than you would like. It fixes the pace for you. But in still water you can be your own pace setter and it is best, always, to make that pace a slow one. When I'm fishing a bug in placid water, I rarely begin the retrieve until the ring that is caused by the bug striking the surface is about ten feet in diameter. If you hold your pace down to about that rate, you will find that you get more bass than you will if you hurry.

Another thing that cannot be emphasized too strongly is the importance of silence. If you are wading, go slowly and quietly; if you are in a boat, avoid loud conversation and sudden noises. The scrape of your shoe or your bait box on the bottom of your boat or the sound of an oar or a paddle striking the gunwale will lose many a good fish for you.

Keeping a bass-bug line afloat and dry always is somewhat of a problem. On a lake or a slow-moving river, it can be done, but where there is any current to speak of you might as well make up your mind that your line is not going to stay on top.

The nylon lines are the answer to the bass-bug fisherman's prayer. When these first came out, I sent one to a New York laboratory and had its specific gravity determined.

Fishing with the Fly Rod

The report came back—.98—two per cent lighter than its equivalent bulk of water. This, of course, means that the line will float awash without the aid of dressing. However, unless the line finish is amply protected by a coat of dressing, it will take on water, sometimes as much as from three to five per cent. This makes the line heavy enough to sink, and the added weight makes itself felt in the casting.

As a base, a new line should be given a rubbed-in coat of waxy dressing, heavily and thoroughly applied and then polished on with a cloth. Then, for added flotation, use one of the greasy dressings, such as Mucelin, on the forward thirty feet of the line, applied liberally over the wax finish. That's the only way I have found to keep a bug line on top for any length of time. When the sun is shining, so that false casting gives rapid drying action, a well-dressed bug line can be kept afloat on still water all day long. Floating a dry-fly line is a relatively simple problem, as it floats quietly without agitation. However, a bass bug must be played to make it effective. Each twitch of the line tends to break the surface tension and pull the line under. When you add current action to this, your line will stay on top only for a short time. If it has been well waterproofed, however, it will not take on weight but will float awash and pick up and cast easily. I always take two or three lines with me when I'm fishing a river. Then if one of them becomes somewhat waterlogged I can put on a fresh one.

This matter of line flotation has definite bearing on the selection of bass bugs. In the current of a bass river, where your line pulls under rather quickly, bugs with high flotation are essential. On a lake or a slow-moving stream, deer-hair lures are both effective and practical. On the moving surface of a river current, these same lures "drown" in a comparatively short time. For this reason I seldom use deer-hair lures in the upper Delaware. There the bugs with cork heads or cork bodies are by far the most satisfactory. Even these must be selected according to conditions. A cork-bodied bug that floats high is apt to "skip" on quiet water, whereas in moving water it plays perfectly because the downward pull of line and leader cuts down its high flotation. By the same token, a cork-bodied bug that plays perfectly on still water is quite likely to pull under in moving water. It is best to have your bugs graded for degree of flotation so that you have your live-water bugs and your still-water bugs.

When you are using deer-hair bugs, it is a good idea to have several of the same pattern. Catching a fish will drown a deer-hair lure, at least temporarily, thereby cutting down its flotation. Thus, rather than waste valuable time trying to reclaim a soaked bug, it is better to remove it from the leader and hang it on the gunwale or in your hatband to dry. We use Joe Messinger's hair frogs a great deal as these little masterpieces are looked upon with favor by the big Smallmouths of the North Branch. We dress these lures with a floatant before we use them, and as soon as we catch a bass with one of them we remove it from the leader and tie on a fresh one. The wet one soon dries in the hot sun.

For fishing the "back-behind" places of a Largemouth lake, a weedless bug is in a class by itself. For this job, the cork-bodied bug is best. Not only is it large and very light in weight, but the cork serves as an excellent anchorage for the weed guard. While there are plenty of weedless bugs on the market, you need not bother to encumber your kit with duplicate sets of bass bugs, as any cork-bodied bug can be "deweeded" satisfactorily in the space of a few minutes. All you need to do the job is an E string for a guitar and a pair of pliers. Lacking wire cutters, a file or even a small stone from the shore will make enough of an indentation in the wire to enable you to break it simply by bending it repeatedly.

Fishing with the Fly Rod

With bugs that have cork heads or cork bodies, the method is simple. First, push the wire into the bottom of the cork head, as close to the eye of the hook as is practical. Keep on pushing until the wire comes through the top of the cork head. Next, bend the wire into a U shape, with the short leg of the U about a quarter of an inch long. Now, push this U back into the cork. This will anchor the wire.

This done, it is a simple matter to bend the wire back until it forms a weed guard below the point of the hook. Cut

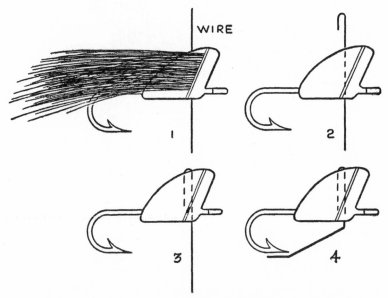

Easy way to place a weedless attachment on a bass bug

it or break it off about even with the bend of the hook. That's all there is to it. With deer-hair bugs, the wire can be secured by wrapping it through and around the eye of the hook, and the weed guard can then be bent into place.

Lacking wire, there is a makeshift weedless gear that will serve fairly well. Simply loop a small rubber band over the head of the bug, so that it rests over the shank of the hook behind the eye, and then stretch the band over the barb of the hook. A glance at the accompanying sketch will show you what I mean. This method is not as satisfactory as the wire weed guard, but it will serve in an emergency.

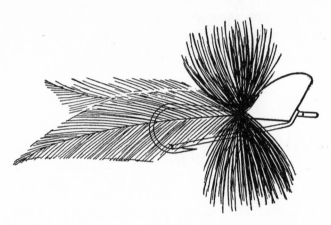

In case you don't have any wire handy, a bass bug can be made fairly weedless with a rubber band. Loop it over the shank of the hook behind the eye and stretch over the barb of the hook.

It is surprising how few men fish weedless bugs or, for that matter, carry them in their bass kits. Even if they do carry them, not very many men know how to use them. The technique is not only quite simple but very productive, both in bass and in excitement.

One of my angling friends, who lives in a city not far from here, is an ardent bass fisherman. With a fly rod and a white marabou streamer he is indeed a finished performer; the havoc he creates annually among the Smallmouth of northern Pennsylvania and southern New York State is now a matter of substantial record. Being a sound conservationist, he returns a high percentage of his catches to the water, but

Fishing with the Fly Rod

he certainly does manage to "educate" an impressive number of bass during the course of each season.

One summer, while we were fishing one of New York State's finger lakes, we encountered hot windless weather which drove the bass down too deep for good fly fishing. Seeing no prospect of any sport with the Smallmouth, we drove over to a Largemouth lake. This lake, being a summer resort, is hard-fished throughout the entire season. Each day its lovely shore lines are combed and hammered with all sorts of bass lures. While the lake is not "fished out," the supply of shore-line bass certainly is depleted to the point where at best only mediocre fishing could be expected. I watched boat after boat move along the shore lines, jockeying for the choice locations. I noticed, however, that not a single boat ventured back behind the shore lines to explore the pockets in the extensive swampy area that makes up about a third of the lake's perimeter. I spoke of this to my friend and, to my surprise, he expressed doubt that the swampy section could be fished. Accordingly, I pulled the boat over to the edge of the swamp and gave him his first lesson in pocket fishing.

First, I had him take down his little streamer rod and set up a big ten-foot affair that he had brought with him. This I fitted out with one of my heavy forward-taper lines, complete with a heavy nine-foot leader and a weedless bass bug— a white Bulldozer. Then I told him to cast the bug back into a hopeless tangle of brush, downed trees, and marsh growth, just as far as he could throw it. He gave me rather a dubious glance, but he did as I told him.

"There she is," he said after the bug had come to rest in a brush pile about seventy feet from the boat. "You'll never get that bug out of there without a hand ax."

"All right," I replied, "now, walk it out."

"What do you mean, 'walk it out'?"

Black Bass

"Lower your rod tip until it points at the bug. Now—strip in line, slowly, about six inches at a time, and let the slack line coil on the bottom of the boat. If you are careful and take your time, the bug will walk right out to you."

He did as I told him and, to his surprise, the bug began to make its way back to him, climbing over twigs, branches, rushes, and logs, now in the water, now in the air. Sure enough, before long it was back close enough to be picked up safely. Then we went fishing. Never have I seen a kid at a circus have more fun than he did that afternoon. He raised bass, big bass and plenty of them. Some he failed to hook, some he lost, and some he managed to land. From two in the afternoon until the mosquitoes drove us in at dusk I handled the boat and watched him have the time of his life. Now and then I'd offer a suggestion, but he's a good fisherman and he didn't need much coaching. I can't recall having seen anybody, man, woman, or child, have more fun. And this, mind you, in a lake that undergoes unusually heavy fishing pressure.

The area where the weedless bass bug comes into its own is in the back-water sloughs of the upper Mississippi, particularly in the general vicinity of Prairie du Chien, Wisconsin. The great majority of these sloughs are blessed with a heavy surface covering of duckwort or duckweed. If you are not familiar with this growth, first impressions may lead you to conclude that it is an unwholesome layer of green slime of some sort. Close inspection, however, reveals that it is really an attractive little plant, complete with roots, stem, leaves, and blossom. Some of the Mississippi sloughs have a solid covering of this weed, but in the majority of the back-waters the duckwort beds are confined to the shore lines. These beds, as you can well imagine, furnish ideal cover for the bass.

Fishing the duckwort beds is an art in itself, one that is

Fishing a bass bug along a shore line in Big Pine Creek, Pennsylvania. We always try to maintain a respectful distance between ourselves and the bass.

Dick, aged sixteen, fishing a shore line in the upper Delaware.

Fishing with the Fly Rod

best learned under the guidance of an experienced Mississippi fisherman, I was lucky in having as my instructors Lyman Howe, newspaper publisher, the late Eric Moir, local fish and game warden, and that kingpin of Mississippi anglers, Z.D. Brown; all these men are of Prairie du Chien.

For fishing the duckwort beds satisfactorily, your terminal tackle should be carefully chosen and assembled. Because flotation is secondary, it is best to use a bug with a small, rounded head which will not pick up the tiny weeds across its face. The wings should be spread, so that they cast a good shadow, such as a large moth might make, and the entire bug should be as weedless as it is possible to make it. Nylon leaders, with as few knots as possible, are the order of the day and these are best fastened to your line by means of interlocking loops and not by a jam knot or a figure eight. Duckwort is tiny stuff, and the smallest projection will pick up a lump of it in short order.

Instead of being cast to the edge of the bed, the bug is cast well in toward shore. Then it is "walked" out over the surface of the bed toward the outer edge. The trick is for the angler to have the bug make its way across the bed much in the same fashion that some luckless insect might employ. Z.D. Brown used to call this process "making the bug talk." The bass who live under the bed as often as not can't see the bug itself—only the disturbance it causes among the miniature weeds and the shadow it casts. Those duckwort bass must like green salad with their meals; when they strike they engulf not only the bug but a big mouthful of duckwort as well.

Another thing that the angler must learn is to "read the beds" to determine probable thickness. Near shore they have a yellowish tone, indicating a depth of weed that is too thick to permit the shadow of the bug to show through. The outer edge of the bed takes on a color of brilliant green. These are the younger plants, too small and sparse to support the weight of the bug. Pay dirt of the bed is the part that is colored a pale olive green. This area is thick enough to support the weight of the bug but not dense enough to prevent the shadow from showing through. It is here that you are apt to raise most of your bass. As often as not, when fishing the duckwort beds, the entire cast and retrieve can be made without having any portion of your terminal tackle come in contact with the water. It makes interesting and absorbing fishing.

When it comes to fishing streamer flies or bucktails, there are two schools of thought among the fly-rod fishermen—those who use spinners or spoons with their streamers and those who do not. I suppose that nine men out of every ten prefer to use a small spoon as an attractor to liven up the action of a streamer fly. However, the tenth man, who scorns spinners, will bring in catches of bass that surely do substantiate his beliefs.

When all is said and done, it boils down to comparative techniques and angling abilities. The fellow who uses a spinner-and-fly combination usually is content to cast his lure out across the current and then let the current and the small spoon do the work for him. In other words, he doesn't have to know a great deal about fishing. On the other hand, the antispinner man is, of necessity, a finished performer; at least, I've never seen one who wasn't. He is a good caster—he has to be to catch bass that way—and he has learned to handle his lure in such a way that it is bound to produce. Two such men come to mind—Dr. Edgar Burke of Jersey City, and Mr. John Woodhull of Elmira, New York. The first time I saw the former in action on a bass river, I watched him hook, land, and release twenty-seven river Smallmouth. Instead of being cut to pattern, as is the method of the average spinner-and-fly fisherman, his technique was varied to meet conditions as he found them. Using a black and white bucktail, he would cast to the shore line, across current. The retrieve was made by stripping in line, about eighteen inches at a time, in decisive jerks that brought the fly through the water in an erratic and evidently irresistible manner. Sometimes he fished it near the surface, sometimes deep, exploring the possibilities of boulders and bottom cover. It was an instructive and interesting thing to watch.

John Woodhull uses much the same technique. His standard lure is his Marabass fly, a creation of white marabou, about three inches long. You will find it reproduced in color. John uses a forward-taper line, a twelve-foot leader, and he can cast surprisingly long distances. His retrieve is basically the same, stripping in line through the guides, but he gives added action to the streamer by agitating the rod tip. Marabou is wiggly stuff anyway and John's streamer looks for all the world like a swimming minnow, darting through the water as though in flight from danger. He, too, is a finished performer and a spinner added to his terminal gear would serve only to cut down the length of his cast, thus reducing the scope of his operations, and also to destroy the illusion that he creates with his adept handling of the fly. Not long ago, in three hours' time, he extracted from the North Branch nine Smallmouth, six of which together tipped the scales at exactly twenty-two pounds. The largest weighed almost five pounds. Most folks agree that spinner-and-fly combinations produce mostly small fish. That definitely is not the case with Dr. Burke or John Woodhull or, for that matter, any other of the antispinner group who knows how to handle his tackle.

As is the case with the plug casters, light-tackle fans are showing up among the ranks of the bass-bug fishermen. In the color plate showing deer-hair lures you will find a concoction called "The Deacon." This is an extra-light lure that can be handled very well with medium-weight trout tackle. Already it has a well-deserved reputation as a fish getter. Fred Geist's "Powderpuff," in its present form, is a

Black Bass

little too much on the bushy, bulky side to qualify as a light tackle lure, but there is no reason why a light-tackle version of it could not easily be tied.

Along this same general line are the little hair bugs, such as the "Weaver Bug" from Wilkes-Barre, Pennsylvania. In Smallmouth rivers these little lures are tremendously effective. They are fished dry, with standard dry-fly technique. Of a summer evening Dick and I have great success with them in the shallow water of the fans and flats of the upper Delaware. Not only that, but these lures are quite effective along the shallow shore lines most any time of day. Just cast them and let them drift quietly, without motion imparted by the rod tip. Now and then you will take surprisingly large bass on these little bugs.

Of course, there are many times when the bass are not disposed to feed at the surface. Then they rise reluctantly, usually with the typical "smash rise," as often as not refusing the lure at the last moment. That is the time that the little sinking metal lures come in mighty handy—things like the fly-rod Tin Liz, Trixoreno, Drone, Dardevil, Johnson Minnow, and so on. These will sink and play along near the bottom. With them it is best to use a sinking line such as Ashaway's "American Finish." Cast them into comparatively deep water, let them sink well down, and retrieve them slowly and erratically, keeping the rod tip down rather close to the water and stripping in line through the guides.

Now and then, when fortune favors you, it is possible to apply orthodox dry-fly methods to your bass fishing. In our Eastern bass rivers, particularly in Pennsylvania, New York, and Maryland, there are a great many hatches of Mayflies that come on the water during the summer evenings of July, August, and even early September. These vary in size from tiny things, size 18 or 20, to the big two-inch Mayfly drakes. Mostly their colors are tan, pale cream, and white. In the

Fishing with the Fly Rod

wadable streams, such as the upper Delaware, we take our positions in the shallow flats or the fans, just above the riffles, and there we wait for the hatch to develop. To facilitate casting long distances, we use big rods and extra-long leaders, fifteen to as much as eighteen feet. As the hatch develops, the fish begin to cruise about the shallows, picking up the flies from the surface. Usually even an approximation of the hatch will be taken readily by the cruising bass, and we really have ourselves a time. In the course of a good evening we can sometimes pick up a dozen good bass apiece. As I say, we keep very few, but we do have fun catching them.

In the big rivers, such as the North Branch, our technique is somewhat different. Sometimes we fish the lower ends of the long pools, keeping the boat upstream from the shallow water of the fans, and moving quietly back and forth across the river. The better way, however, is to anchor the boat about midstream in one of the smooth-water runs, just below the riffles. We learn from previous observation about the most advantageous place to locate the boat. Then we wait for the fun to begin.

If the hatch proves to be a good one (as it usually does in the North Branch), just about every bass in the pool moves up into the riffles to feed—not only the small fish but the old tackle busters as well. That is one of the few times of the year that these big fellows are readily available to the fly-rod fishermen. These big fish, being creatures of habit, always take up their feeding locations in the same places every evening. Thus, it is time well spent to locate, for future reference, several of these spots. Dick and I have had some hair-raising evenings, fishing these Mayfly hatches. With the small hooks which we have to use to match the drifting hatch, about the best we have been able to land is around the four-pound mark but we have hooked, fought, and lost monsters of fully double that weight. On one of the big rivers, don't make the mistake of trying to row a boat or paddle a canoe around one of these feeding runs. About all you will accomplish is to put down the feeding fish. Better by far to scout your territory first. Then go back the next evening, anchor your boat, and wait for the fishing to begin.

Strangely enough, in all of our fishing excursions on the bass rivers of many states, we have never seen one single fisherman availing himself of the top-notch dry-fly fishing to be found there. That, to me, is a surprising thing, but the fact remains that it is true.

One August evening, not so long ago, a friend and I were driving home from a day of fishing in the North Branch. Unfortunately the ladies of our choice had issued ultimatums, demanding our return in time for the festivities that had been planned for that evening. As we drove across the bridge, we saw that there was a copious hatch of big Mayfly drakes over the pool, so we parked the car and walked back on the bridge to watch the show. To be sure, we were late getting home and, severally and collectively, we caught a little hell from our irate better halves, but what we saw was worth it.

I have always maintained that the bait fishermen of the North Branch do not do a great deal of harm to the static supply of adult bass in that river. That evening went a long way to substantiate my opinion. By actual count there were over thirty-five boats tied up along the shores of that pool and the banks are lined with summer camps. Yet here in the water below us were hundreds of full-size adult Smallmouth, literally stuffing themselves with Mayflies. Some of them were of such ample size that the initial swirl after the tipup rise was larger than the top of a hogshead.

One boat was out, occupied by a single fisherman. He was drifting down through the pool, a rod extending out from each side of the boat. Now and again he would lift a rod, recast his bait, and allow it to sink once more to the bottom.

Fishing with the Fly Rod

All around him were rising bass, taking Mayflies and cruising about near the surface, leaving wakes behind them like so many motor boats. To these he paid not the slightest attention. He may not have been catching any fish, but, by God, he was fishin'! As I say, bass fishermen learn slowly.

CHAPTER 11

General Discussion

WHEN YOU VISIT A lake for the first time, it will pay you to devote your first day to the job of learning as much as you can about it. Study the topography of the surrounding country, as this will help you locate the springholes. Investigate the shore lines. These and, of course, the offshore bars and reefs are the feeding areas. You can't know too much about them.

In the northern lakes, deep shore lines that have ample cover are excellent places to look for Smallmouth. These fish, as we mentioned earlier, prefer a sixty-seven-degree temperature if they can find it. Thus, you don't find them along shallow shore lines unless they happen to be cruising in search of food.

If you can find some offshore weed beds, where the water is deep, say twelve or fifteen feet, as a rule you will find Smallmouth there also. Weed beds are good feeding areas and they provide excellent cover. In Lake Memphremagog, Vermont, the offshore weed beds are notorious spots for big Smallmouth, as are the bars, reefs, and small islands. Except for a few stretches where the shore lines are quite deep, the really good fishing in that lake is offshore.

Inlets and springholes or deep shore lines that have a trickle of spring seepage usually are concentration spots. Frequently

General Discussion

the topography of the bordering country will guide you to these places.

If the lake is a big one, the wind will set up currents in it from day to day. Then it is a good plan to investigate the passes or "thoroughfares" between the islands. There is one of these in Big Lake, near Grand Lake Stream, Maine. The bottom of this pass is composed of ledge rock on the upcurrent side (if that's the word). This ledge drops off into deep black water, and always there is a school of big bass lying just under the ledge, waiting for what the current may bring them. A sinking lure that is cast up over the ledge and allowed to sink as the current drifts it over the edge seldom completes its journey without complications with a heavy bass.

A good guide can save you a great deal of time and effort in locating the choice fishing. He has learned, from past experience, where a great many of the concentration spots are to be found. He knows the inlets and the spring feeders and, usually, the springholes. It being his job to find fishing for you, he must, if he wishes to have continuous employment, know something about these places. However, what he doesn't know—at least, I've never found one who did—is the temperature setup of his lake. It is up to you to find that out for yourself.

The study of fresh-water lakes and ponds is one of the sciences. Limnology it is called, and while it deals with all the biological and physiological aspects of the matter, it concerns itself largely with temperature studies, as these have great bearing on the other two.

Lake temperatures arrange themselves into a rather set pattern, year after year. When the ice first goes out in the spring, water temperatures in a lake are pretty much the same from top to bottom. It doesn't take very long for the warm spring days to assert themselves. Then, if the weather is not too windy, temperatures arrange themselves into three separate layers. The *Epilimnion* or upper layer is a shallow affair,

Black Bass

rarely more than three or four feet deep, composed of comparatively warm water. In small ponds or dams, unaffected by the wind, I have seen this upper layer actually confined to from six to eight inches of depth. In this layer the temperatures from top to bottom show very little change. The *Hypolimnion*, or bottom layer, comprises the very great majority of the water in a lake. Like the upper layer, there is little variation in temperature from top to bottom. Between these two layers lies the cushioning layer, in which temperatures undergo a rapid change, from warm water on top to cold

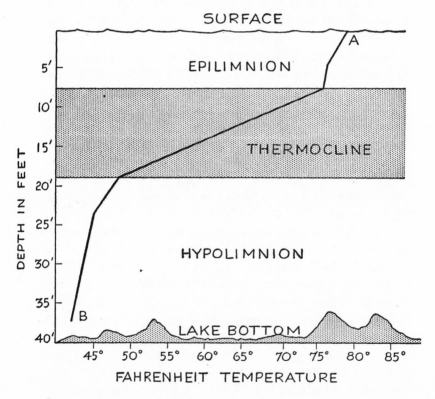

Cross section of typical layer arrangement of lake temperatures during the summer months

General Discussion

water on the bottom. This is called the *Thermocline* ("temperature slope" would be a rather free translation), and this in-between layer has decided influence on the aquatic life of any lake.

Comparatively recent studies have disclosed that the Hypolimnion or lower layer is frequently deficient in oxygen content. This is not always true, but sometimes there are deep "pockets," lacking in spring-water seepage and too deep and sheltered for turnover by wind or current action, in which shallow-water fish, such as minnows on a bait hook, have difficulty in living. While this condition is far from being the general rule, as is amply attested by the fact that such fish as lake trout, ling, smelt, and so on prefer the deep waters during the summer months, it does exist now and then.

In your bass fishing, particularly for Smallmouth, this Thermocline should be taken into account. Wind and currents play an important part in determining its depth and the only way to find out what is going on, temperature wise, is to take with you a maximum and minimum thermometer and learn for yourself at about what level the Smallmouth are finding the temperatures they prefer. Fasten a string to your thermometer, lower it over the side, and see at what depth the sixty-seven-degree level happens to be for that day. That way you can locate the probable depth of the offshore concentrations.

This same thermometer will come in handy in locating springholes and seepage spots. Without it, you can only guess at probable temperatures; with it, you can be sure. In your offshore fishing the same holds true. Bars and shoals that sometimes are well populated with bass, now and then will be deserted. Take your thermometer along and you can find out why and, more important, at what depths to look for your fish.

In a made lake it is a good plan to know the location of the stream bed. Artificial lakes, for the most part, are created by erecting a dam and impounding the waters of a stream. Even after the dam is full the flow of cold water from the inlet continues to move through the same old channel. If you happen to be addicted to trolling, than which there is no more unexciting or inept way to fish, probably your best bet for Smallmouth will be to follow this channel.

Finding Largemouth in a lake is comparatively easy when compared with locating good Smallmouth fishing. Thermoclines don't concern a Largemouth a great deal. So long as he has good cover, an adequate food supply, and enough water to cover him comfortably, he isn't bothered a whole lot by temperatures. After all, he's a warm-water fish and as such can be quite happy in high temperatures. Now and then he will make his home along a deep-water shore line—a spot where you would naturally expect to find Smallmouth—but mostly he prefers the shallows.

As stated earlier, not all the Largemouth in a lake live along shore and there is always a reserve supply schooled up in the open water, but enough of them do make their homes in the shallows to keep us happy. For these fish, I think that your time is best spent with a surface lure. Not that they won't take underwater lures. They will. But they take surface lures just about as readily—sometimes even more readily—and the explosive strike of a Largemouth is one of the greatest thrills in bass fishing.

No matter whether you are fishing a weed bed for Largemouth or for Smallmouth, it has always seemed to me that best results are obtained with sinking lures. I am talking now about the offshore, deep-water weed beds. For some reason, bass of both varieties seem reluctant to rise through a deep weed bed to strike a surface lure. Oh, sure, some of them will, but your chances are better if you fish deep for them.

In lakes there are three types of hatches that it is well to know—dragon flies, damsel flies, and Mayfly drakes. These are apt to appear on the water most any time. However,

General Discussion

these hatches adhere to the yearly cycle, just as the stream insects do, so it is a smart idea, when you encounter a hatch on any lake, to make a note of the date for future reference if you expect to fish that lake again. For illustration, the tremendous "fish-fly" hatch of Lake Michigan (which actually is a hatch of Mayfly drakes) comes on in mid-July. This hatch is so heavy that windrows of nymph cases form along shore where the surf washes them up on the beaches.

Bass can be superselective when these hatches are on the water, and it is sometimes the devil's own task to find an artificial lure that they will take readily, particularly when there are newly hatched darning needles available. However, it can be done.

Up at Echo Lake, Vermont, we used to have some busy evenings when the big Mayfly drakes were on the water. Then the grown-up Smallmouth would be cruising about, close enough to the surface to leave V-shaped wakes behind them. The trick was to spot an imitation in the path of one of these fish. It took a great deal of rowing and casting but we did manage to hook and land some beautiful bass that way.

Prior to 1940, Dick and I did most of our river fishing in the upper Delaware, usually in the West Branch in the general vicinity of Deposit, New York. This is small water, as bass rivers go, but it is easy wading, good fly fishing, amply supplied with bass, and altogether delightful. Now and then we do manage to extract a big bass from the West Branch, but mostly the fish run about a foot long. When we can't hook and release from thirty to fifty bass a day from those waters, we haven't had very good fishing.

There isn't really very much to learn about fishing small water for bass. The pools that we fish are fairly shallow and the bass will rise readily to a surface lure. Through the long shallow flats we fish both the shore lines and the open water, exploring all the possibilities of obvious cover, such as rocks, boulders, ledges, and so on. All you need for that job is good

Black Bass

tackle, the ability to handle a bass lure at long distances, and a durable casting hand. Fortunately, Dick and I have these things, so we catch more than our share of bass. As I say, we keep very few.

In a bass river, a small one, the fish in the pools generally are located directly in the "thread of the stream"—the feeding lane. If you will watch any pool or flat in a bass river, you will see that the bubbles that come down from the riffles form themselves into a definite line as they move downstream. This line marks the feeding lane. Sometimes there are two lines, but generally these converge, before they have gone very far, into one main line of drift. The fish know that this line of drift carries food as well as bubbles, and that is where they take up their locations. A bass bug or a streamer, cast across this line and played back through it, usually will bring results.

When the bass in a small river are inactive, then comes the time when complete familiarity with the river pays off. In every river there are concentration spots—pockets in the flats, unusual patches of bottom cover, deep spots in the riffles, all sorts of places. For example, in most riffles there are small backwaters that lie between the bank and the fast-water run. These little backwaters—"bath tubs," we call them—are usually covered with foam and nearly always they will hold one or two good bass. Even though the fish in the open water may be inactive, the bass in these odd locations generally are glad to sample anything that chance brings to them. Because of their limited range, they must take or reject anything that looks edible, and they have formed the habit of striking quickly. Normally we don't bother the fish in the "hot spots," but when we want a mess of bass we can usually pick up what we need from these pockets.

Here and there in every river you will find smooth-water runs. These are famous places for bass. We fish them either with surface lures, streamers, or pork-rind lures, and the bass

General Discussion

take one just about as well as the others. A two pounder, with the heavy current to help him, will just about break your arm when he strikes. Runs are always comparatively shallow and the fish do not have to move far to take one of your offerings. Thus, these places rarely disappoint you.

Now and then a deep pool will terminate in a very short fan before the water breaks into the next riffle. Usually the bottom slopes back sharply in a steep drop-off. It is wise to pay extra-careful attention to these places when you find them. Bass are always on the lookout for food that drifts on the surface. Thus, they line up along these drop-offs where they are in position either to feed or to avail themselves of the protection of the deep water directly in front of them. A bass bug or a streamer, cast from above, often will recieve quite a reception.

When I first became acquainted with the North Branch of the Susquehanna River in 1940, fatuously I was under the impression that I knew quite a bit about river fishing for Smallmouth. It didn't take me long to find out that I knew very little. A big Smallmouth river is indeed a great educator in the ways of these fish if a man will keep his eyes open and, more important, his mind. Adult Smallmouth are not easy to catch. They are smart, as fish go, wary, and temperamental. Small things, to which small or medium-sized bass pay not the slightest attention, serve as a warning to the full-grown bass that all is not as it should be. When that happens, they go on a sit-down strike and refuse to have anything to do with artificial lures, or, for that matter, live bait.

There is a stretch of water in the North Branch, about two miles upstream from the town of Wyalusing, which is known as "the Terrytown level." This area is about a mile and a half long, from riffle to riffle, and in it is every type of bass water. After the North Branch bass had deflated my ego to the point of humility, I spent two full seasons in learning what I now know about the vagaries of big-river bass fishing in general and the Terrytown level in particular. Not only that, but the Terrytown bass helped to convince me that I still know all too little about taking adult Smallmouth with anything even savoring of consistency.

The lower end of the Terrytown level is a long, deep pool that shallows off into a broad fan. At the upper end of this mile-long stretch the river bends through about forty-five degrees in a smooth, even curve. Scattered through this upper half mile are deep shore lines, shallow shore lines, smooth-water runs, bars under varying depths of water, seepage spots, spring-feeder inlets—in fact, pretty much every sort of river bass water. To learn all that there is to know about such confusing variety takes time and some doing.

Throughout the lower mile, the shore line on the Wyalusing side of the Terrytown level is impressive. The Lehigh Valley Railroad tracks skirt the river's edge and the embankment has been reinforced with large rock to prevent erosion. This embankment drops off into deep water and it looks, at first glance, like an ideal home for Smallmouth. First impressions sometimes are troublemakers. Not until many weary hours of fruitless casting had been wasted along this shore line did the true situation begin to dawn upon my tardy brain.

As stated above, the river bends through the upper half mile of the Terrytown level. Finally it dawned on us that the shore line ceased to hold bass below the point where the bend gave way to the straight shore line of the pool proper. Above that point the shore-line fishing is good, very good. Below that point, a good bass from the shore line is very much the exception. Careful inspection showed us that the main current swings away from the shore at exactly that spot, leaving a band of dead water about thirty or forty feet wide throughout the length of the pool proper. What looked, at first glance, like ideal Smallmouth territory proved to be suitable mainly for panfish and an odd pickerel. Smallmouth,

The Terrytown Level in the North Branch of the Susquehanna River, near Wyalusing, Pennsylvania.

Standard equipment for 99 per cent of the river fishermen of Pennsylvania and New York: a steel "pole," a pail of live bait, and an anchored boat.

General Discussion

as I said earlier, like live water. So look over your shore lines before you waste valuable time. If the water is fairly deep and flows clean and fresh right up to the pebbles at the water's edge, there you will probably find your adult bass.

The embankment throughout the area where the river bends has been fortified against damage by masonwork in the form of large stone blocks, extending from lowwater mark clear to the top of the bank. This, too, drops off into deep water. Through the simple expedient of fishing its entire length time after time, we learned that certain parts of this bank were more productive than others. Wondering about this, I took time out to study the topography of the country behind the railroad embankment. Sure enough, directly opposite the stretch where we found our best fishing there was a fold in the hills which drained into a spring-fed marsh. This, so far as we could determine, had no outlet save to seep through under the railroad embankment. Investigation with the thermometer showed that this conclusion was correct.

Directly upstream, probably as drainage from the marsh, a small spring bubbles out from the bank and exhausts perhaps five or ten gallons of cold water per minute into the river. One day, during the course of a Solunar Period, I cast a bass bug so that it landed almost at the mouth of this tiny feeder. The water being rather shallow at this point, we had thought it wise to keep the boat well away from shore, as big bass take alarm all too easily. Thus, I was using an extra-long line. To my surprise, an old whopper of a bass darted away from the mouth of the feeder. He must have been lying in water that barely covered his dorsal fin. Evidently he was startled rather than alarmed, because we saw him circle back to see what had disturbed him. He made no move to take the bug as the current carried it away—merely swam about looking at it. Just for luck, I picked up the bug, timed my cast carefully, and let go again. By great good fortune, the bug landed in exactly the same spot. This time Mr. Bass didn't

Black Bass

hesitate; instead, he fell upon it like a wolf. My partner shot the boat into deep water and the war was on. After twenty minutes of rugged resistance we netted him. He was a beautiful fish—almost two feet long and just a few ounces short of the five-pound mark.

Several miles upstream in this same river there is a long pool known as Echo Beach. Why the name, I don't know. Repeated shoutings have disclosed no echo to speak of, and the beach is pretty much the same sort of riverbank that you can find along any pool of the North Branch—small rocks, pebbles, and mud. Anyway, that's its name and it turns up some pretty high-class bass fishing for us. At the upper end of this pool is the smooth-water run where Dick and I have had so many entanglements with old tackle busters when we have been fishing dry fly during the Mayfly hatches.

At the lower end of this run there has been built up a pebbly bar that extends perhaps a hundred yards down into the pool. The current of the run spills over this bar, keeping the water behind it fresh and alive, and it is a great place for big bass to congregate. Here it was that I showed one of our confirmed bait fishermen more big bass in one afternoon than he would see normally in a month of bait fishing. We were fishing with Joe Messinger's little hair frogs at the time, and we raised and hooked eighteen big bass in the space of three hours. These fish lay both along shore and just under the bar. That day the bass staged a performance that I have never been able to explain. The fish along shore, when they rose to the bug, came up with a tipup rise, ending in a swirl as the bass turned to go back to his location. Not so the fish under the bar. These took with a rush and a flurry of spray that sent tingles along your backbone and placed heavy strain on tackle and wrist. One rise was exactly like the last, yet the bar and the shore are not more than forty or fifty yards apart. Incidentally, this same bar is a wonderful place for big walleyed pike—the Susquehanna Salmon—and the bait fishermen who know about it profit greatly by their knowledge.

The lower end of the Echo Beach pool shallows off into what, in the Delaware country, is known as a "niggerhead flat" or "niggerhead eddy." In case you're wondering, a "niggerhead" is a round boulder on the stream bottom. Thus, a "niggerhead flat" is a stretch of fairly shallow water that is studded with oversize boulders, rounded off by years of erosion. This type of bottom cover makes an ideal home for Smallmouth. There being a certain amount of weed growth among the rocks, which, of course, shelters plenty of bottom life and minnows, an area of this sort provides both food and safe cover. As a rule the shore lines of a niggerhead flat are shallow barren affairs, but out in the main current a man can spend many profitable hours either with fly rod or with casting rod. The Bass Mine in the upper Delaware is just such a spot. It pays to take your time in a place like this, as every rock is apt to shelter a good bass.

As in small rivers, a big river usually has quite a few deep pools which terminate in sharp drop-offs and short shallow fans. Fish these drop-offs at a respectful distance from the upstream side as they usually hold extra-large fish.

A noteworthy exception to the live-water rule in a bass river is the spring-fed cove. In the Delaware these are called "binnacles," goodness knows why. They are definitely backwaters, with no current to speak of, but they are springfed, cold, and deep, and the bass like them. One summer a friend of mine, who had been tipped off by a native of the valley to fish the binnacles, was devoting very special care and time to these cold-water coves. It so happened that he was fishing with a doctor, but in the interest of efficiency they had decided to use two boats. He cast a big number-two bass fly into a likely-looking binnacle and it was taken immediately by a large bass. When the big fish felt the hook, he dashed across the cove, placing heavy strain on the rod, and then jumped.

Black Bass

The fly pulled free while the fish was in the air and the spring of the rod brought it sailing back to imbed itself, clear over the barb, in the end of my friend's rather prominent nose.

My friend clipped the leader and then rowed downriver to get help from his doctor companion, feeling sure that he would know some magic method of painless removal and subsequent antisepsis.

The doctor was first surprised and then interested.

"Hm," he said, "clear over the barb. Let me have a close look."

Unsuspecting, my friend held still while the doctor, using his best bedside manner, looked at the fly, the while taking a firm grip with thumb and forefinger. Without warning, he yanked, hard. The fly came free, part of my friend's nose adhering to the barb, and blood spurted like a fountain. My friend let out a screech like a banshee. Cold water soon stanched the flow of blood and a bandaid completed the treatment.

"There you are," said the doctor. "That'll be all right. Bled itself clean. Go fishing and forget it."

Later that day my friend took the doctor to task for his brutal treatment.

"Walter," said the doctor, "there are two ways to remove a hook. Human flesh is tough stuff. It doesn't let go easily. I could have taken you back to the landing, driven to the nearest hospital or drugstore, anesthetized, operated with a knife, and then sterilized. A messy, painful, time-wasting process. The way I did it was better, any way you look at it."

Just as in a salmon river or a trout stream, fishing in a bass river varies with the water level. Thus, you must gauge your fishing according to conditions. In times of low, clear water, it is a good plan to spend most of your time in the deeper water, as the shallows and flats don't provide enough protection for the fish to move freely. After a rain, when the river

General Discussion

flows fresh and cool, a few inches deeper than before, the shallower water once again will be productive.

In the North Branch there are a great many weed beds. These, to continue to maintain their footing, grow in the quieter water, somewhat removed from the main current. Weeds provide ideal cover for the small creatures of a river and the North Branch weed beds are alive with crawfish, minnows, and insect larvae. When the water is low and clear, the weed beds are not very productive, but after a rain, when the river is up a bit and may be slightly discolored, we have had great success casting a bass bug to their edges.

When a bass strikes and we have him "on the reel" with a tight line, we make it a point to reset the hook to make doubly sure that the barb is driven home. A big bass has strong jaws, equipped with tiny teeth that are set in his big, gristly lips. When he takes a small lure, and this is particularly true of rough lures such as hair bugs and such, he can grip it tight enough so that not even the point will be engaged on the initial strike. Therefore, as soon as we can manage to do so, we take in line until the rod points almost directly at the fish and then "give him the butt" to break his hold on the lure and drive the barb home. I have talked to several experienced bass fishermen about this "second set," and all agree that it is a good idea. True, now and then a lightly hooked fish will be set free in this way, but the chances are that he would throw the hook anyway. By and large, I believe that a great deal more good than harm is done by resetting the hook as soon as possible after the strike.

Black bass, Largemouth or Smallmouth, whether they are in a river or a lake, have a set daily cycle of feeding activity and rest periods. You've seen it happen. Bass will strike to beat the band for an hour or so. Then, gradually, the activity quiets down until at last you find no takers for your offerings. These bursts of feeding may happen almost any time of day or night. Up until twenty-odd years ago, fishing through one of

Black Bass

these activity periods was largely a matter of guesswork or good luck. The best thing to do was to start fishing early in the morning and fish right through until dusk, taking your fish as they happened to come. Today we are somewhat more fortunate.

Seventy-five or a hundred years ago, Southern market hunters used to plan their forays into the wilds according to the rule of "moon up–moon down." In other words, they learned that when the moon was directly overhead or directly underfoot were the best times for fishing or shooting. Then all wildlife was active and in evidence. Probably they learned it from the Indians. Subsequent inquiry has disclosed that the Indians knew of this feeding cycle, at least some of the tribes did.

Back in the winter of 1925–26, I first learned of this rule of wildlife behavior from Bob Wall (whom I mentioned earlier), who operated a fishing camp on the upper St. Johns River, Florida. No need here to go into the development of the theory, the mistakes, and the eventual solution. Suffice to say that I applied modern science to an old bit of folklore and came up with a schedule of daily feeding and activity periods that has proven itself under the infallible test of time. For convenience, the theory is called the Solunar Theory and the feeding and activity periods are called Solunar Periods. The word "Solunar" is a convenience term, coined from the words "solar" and "lunar." The Solunar Periods, for each day of the year, are published annually in book form, or you can find the weekly Solunar schedule in the newspapers of most of the important cities of the United States and Canada. So much for that.

While I was working out a satisfactory method to determine, a year in advance, the schedule of Solunar Periods, I noticed that there was a feeding flurry of somewhat shorter duration than the moon up–moon down periods, which came about midway between the longer periods. Thus, Solunar

General Discussion

Periods have been divided into major periods and minor periods. Don't make the mistake of regarding the minor periods as being of little importance. They are so christened merely to differentiate the time factors, the minor periods usually lasting about half as long as the major ones.

During Solunar Periods, fish display two prominent characteristics besides increased activity. One is a pronounced lack of fear or caution at these times; the other is a decided tendency to feed at the surface. There is no present explanation for these things. However, we know about them and we may as well put them to good use.

Under ordinary conditions, a full-grown adult bass wouldn't dream of swimming about in the shallows, thus exposing himself to his natural enemies. During an active Solunar Period, however, he will cruise around in broad daylight, sometimes in water that barely covers him, entirely oblivious to the fact that he is a sitting duck for any osprey that happens to come along. Many times I have seen schools of large bass, evidently in from deep water, moving along shallow shore lines not over two feet deep. When the fish are behaving this way is the ideal time to fish the fans. On the average, these shallows hold more big bass than any other waters. We've had some nerve-wrecking times across the fans during Solunar Periods and, incidentally, we've taken many able bass that way. Also, this is the time that the big boys move into the smooth-water feeding runs at the tails of the riffles.

In the summer of 1942, when Dick and I were fishing in Wisconsin, we encountered an excellent instance of the behavior of bass during Solunar Periods and at other times. Because of heavy rains, the rivers were unfishable, so our guide took us to a lake in Northern Wisconsin called Deer Lake. The shore lines of this lake were beautiful—deep enough, plenty of cover of all sorts, and altogether delightful. When I saw the lake, I started fishing with high hopes.

My guide for the day was a Forest Ranger who, I learned

Black Bass

later, had a low opinion of outdoor writers. However, he had been told by the big boss to show us the best the country afforded, so he was doing his job.

Deer Lake is about four miles long and a mile wide. We started down the best-looking shore line, Ed keeping the boat about forty feet from shore. After a hundred yards or so of no strikes, I suggested that we might be fishing them a bit close.

"Mebbe so," said Ed. "How far kin you throw that thing?"

I replied somewhat to the effect that I could "throw" it about as far as he could cast a plug. He looked at me with disbelief but we moved away from shore. Then, gradually, it dawned upon me that I was being put to the test. The distance between the boat and shore continued to increase slightly as we moved along. Seventy, eighty, ninety feet, he really put me up against it. For half a mile I fished the distances he set, placing my bug up into the choice spots and saying not a word. At last Ed broke the silence.

"All right, mister. You win. That's the by-Goddest job o' casting I ever see. Lemme look at that outfit."

I passed him my rod and he inspected rod, line, reel, leader, and bug with evident knowledge and appreciation. At last he handed it back without comment and we went on with our fishing.

Evidently conditions were entirely against us. Try as I would, I could not raise so much as one single bass. I tried many shapes, colors, and varieties. No good. After several hours we reached the end of the lake. I looked at my watch and saw that a major Solunar Period was scheduled to arrive right about then.

The lower end of Deer Lake is flanked by several attractive summer homes, and the shore is a gently sloping beach of white sand. Except for the places where the summer residents had cleared the beach for swimming, this sandy slope was

General Discussion

covered with a rather scattered growth of rushes—"toolies," Ed called them.

"Lots o' times the bass work in outa deep water to feed along here of an evenin'. Let's give her a whirl," he told me.

Accordingly he placed the boat in position, just nice casting range from the edge of the growth of rushes. I looked at my watch again. Sure enough—time for that Solunar Period. I fished as Ed wished me to, but still no takers. While I fished, I watched the rushes. I thought I detected movement here and there, back in where the rushes grew more thickly, but I wasn't sure. Then my suspicions were confirmed. A big bass slashed savagely through a school of minnows, way back in close to shore, and the luckier members of the school scattered through the air in all directions in their frantic bid for existence. At once I reeled in line, clipped off the bug I had been using, and tied on a cork-bodied bug that was equipped with a weed guard. Then I told Ed to shove the boat right up into the rushes.

"Shucks, mister, you can't fish back in there. Get hung up every cast, sure as shootin'."

I said we probably would but let's try it anyway, so Ed pushed the boat in as I had suggested. I waited until I saw the rushes move, about sixty feet from the boat. Then I cast the bug where the bass would be sure to see it. When I started to "walk it out" through the rushes I found that it touched water only now and then. Most of the time it was in the air, climbing over the wind-blown reeds. It had not gone more than four or five feet, however, before the bass spied it. Socko! He nailed it while it was a good foot above the water.

We fished up and down that bed of rushes for a good two hours. Evidently the place was a favorite feeding area for the offshore fish, as new customers kept moving in constantly. They were mostly big fish, three pounds and up, and we had the time of our lives. We raised fish, plenty of fish. We missed them, hooked them, lost some, and landed some. I honestly think that Ed had as much fun as I did. When the Solunar Period passed and the area had become quiet once more, we paddled back up the lake to join the other boat. It was one of the most clean-cut examples of Solunar activity and non-Solunar inactivity I have ever seen.

When I returned home, I sent Ed a medium-priced bug rod and a nylon forward-taper line. Here's hoping that he put them to good use.

Earlier in this book I have talked about the evident preference for surface lures that bass display during Solunar Periods. However, it is important enough to bear repetition. Surface lures during Solunar Periods, underwater lures at other times; that is the rule that we follow in the bass rivers and in the Largemouth lakes. To some extent it applies also in the lakes where Smallmouth live, but there it is affected by the depth of the Thermocline. If the fish lie too deep, underwater lures are indicated regardless of Solunar Periods.

During some twenty-odd years of fussing around with Solunar periods and their effects, I have made it my business to check up on record catches. By "record catches" I mean both record fish and record numbers of fish. Some of the data on these catches have been easy to come by. Often, however, it has required not a little correspondence to get the information I wanted. In all, I suppose that I have run down approximately two hundred instances and their supporting data. To my surprise, and, incidentally, pleasure, better than 95 per cent of these record catches have three things in common. They were made during the warm summer months; they were made during the three days of the dark of the moon, most of them at midday; and, last but most important, they were made during Solunar Periods. This information can be important in your bass fishing if you wish to put it to good use. A glance at the Solunar Tables will show you that the major Solunar Periods during this phase of the moon occur

General Discussion

at noon or shortly thereafter and again at midnight or in the small hours of the morning.

Now, every bass fisherman is hoping for big fish every time he goes out. Well, that's the time to get the big boys. The fact that the major Solunar Period comes at noon on a hot July day does not alter the fact that the big bass will be moving and on the feed at that time. So, plan your fishing trips to take full advantage of the Solunar Periods. Your sport will profit from this habit.

Of course, there is usually good fishing at daybreak and again at dusk. Those are the times when the day shift lays off and the night shift goes to work, or vice versa. But these times are of comparatively short duration. Keep track of the Solunar Periods and you won't be sorry.

A great many people place a lot of faith in the apogee and perigee phases of the moon in determining the probable quality of their fishing. To save you the trouble of looking up "apogee" and "perigee," these are two stages of the moon in its orbit. When the moon is in apogee, it is then at its farthest distance from the earth. When the moon is in perigee, it is than at its closest point to the earth. The theory is that fish are more active through the perigee stage and for several days thereafter.

While a great many states have placed a ban on night fishing, there are still a goodly number that have not, so maybe we'd better talk about that a bit while we're at it. In the first place, the shore lines aren't very productive during the dark hours. I don't know why this should be, but it is true. In the dark, it is all right if you use the shore line as a guide, but you will do better if you devote most of your attention to the open water, ten, fifteen or twenty feet out from shore. Also, the shallows and the flats are quite productive after dark. Don't move about much or make any noise. Better stand still or anchor your boat, and let the fish come to you. If you are fishing a shore line, keeping well out,

Black Bass

don't lift your paddle from the water. Feather the blade between strokes, and move slowly, quietly, and without conversation.

While underwater lures will catch fish after dark, my preference is for surface lures. The fish take them readily and the fuss that a surface lure makes on the water seems to act as an attractor.

Of course, water conditions have a decided bearing on your fishing. During times of low water, the fish tend to be shy and wary and they are hard to catch. In the upper Delaware, that is the time when we usually have to fall back on our knowledge of pockets and concentration spots. After a rain, the fishing is usually good. A rain seems to have a stimulating effect on both lake and river fish. In a river, don't be discouraged if the water is somewhat discolored. One of the best catches I ever brought back from the North Branch was taken when the river was coffee colored—coffee and cream—and visibility couldn't have been more than three feet. We fished the live-water shore lines, and the big bass really were on the prod. Also, you will recall that I mentioned that the river was discolored the first time I fished the Delaware. That day I couldn't see bottom in thigh-deep water, yet I took bass to beat the band. Naturally, if the river is in flood, you might just as well stay home, but normal discoloration after a summer rain usually stimulates the fishing.

Abnormal changes in water level usually have adverse effects. High water levels or low water levels, either in a lake or a river, will often completely ruin the fishing. These unfortunate conditions cause the bass to redistribute themselves and the fishing is bound to suffer under such unnatural circumstances.

Generally speaking, you won't find very good fishing in a lake that is "working" or "purging." This is when the water plants reseed themselves and the green "bloom" places so much extra vegetable matter in suspense that the carbonic-

General Discussion

acid gas content of the water is stepped up from a normal two or three parts to the million to as much as seventeen or eighteen parts. This seems to affect the appetites and feeding habits of the fish, and they take a lure reluctantly. In addition, visibility is cut down appreciably. It's a pretty good idea to stay away from a working lake.

One of the vital factors that can determine the quality of your fishing is the *trend* of the barometer. The word "trend" is emphasized to distinguish it from "level" or "reading." It doesn't really make a whole lot of difference at what level the barometer stands (always excepting, of course, the *abnormal* levels which indicate hurricanes). By and large, it is the trend of the glass that is the deciding factor. If the glass is shaky and dropping slightly, the chances are that your fishing will be poor. Conversely, if the glass is steady or rising, the fishing probably will be good, always providing that other factors, such as water conditions and temperatures, are favorable.

Summer rains, if they are not downpours or cloudbursts, are beneficial. Have you ever noticed that country folks seem to prefer fishing in a light summer rain? The reason is obvious when you stop to take a close look at it. When a summer rain is approaching, the barometer falls. That means that the fish retire to their resting stations to take advantage of safe cover until the disturbance has passed, a good many of them going to deep water.

By the time the rain arrives, the glass will have leveled off or started to rise. Thus, during a light summer rain, the bait fisherman finds a supply of hungry fish waiting for him, all nicely schooled up in the deep pools.

It is difficult to generalize about thunderstorms. A great many people say that thunder spoils the fishing. I have not found this to be true. It has been my good fortune to find good fishing before, during, and after thunderstorms. I have always believed that the quality of the fishing, when there

Black Bass

is a thunderstorm about, depends entirely upon the behavior of the barometer at the time. Unfortunately, thunderstorms are not cut to pattern. They may be twisters—meaning that they revolve about a center as any self-respecting storm should, or they may be rollers—meaning that the disturbance actually does roll its way across country. This, of course, is apt to present a pretty complex pattern of barometric behavior. Having had two friends killed by lightning while fishing in thunderstorms, I now emulate the fish and retire to the safe cover of my automobile until the storm has passed.

Let me remind you again of some of the common errors that are so prevalent among bass fishermen.

First—Don't fish too fast. You may cover more water but you'll catch fewer fish.

Second—Don't fish too close. Bass take alarm more easily than most folks think; at least, big bass do. Fish at a respectful distance.

Third—Don't fish too shallow with your sinking lures. Get them right down next to the bottom where the fish live. If you don't know how fast your lure sinks, drop it over the side (with the line attached) and count slowly as it sinks. You can measure on your line how far it goes in four or five seconds. Then, when you cast, you will know how long to wait before retrieving.

Fourth—Don't make any noise. And this includes loud talk.

Last but not least—Don't forget to sharpen those hooks.

CHAPTER 12

Bait Fishing for Bass

WE MAY JUST as well understand each other right at the start of this chapter. I'll not mince words. Better get things settled right out loud. This is the way things stand with me.

I have absolutely no use for bait fishing.

Maybe I'd better clarify my position regarding live bait. I am *not* a purist. If live bait were the best way to catch bass, I'd probably fish bait exclusively. But it isn't, not by a long shot.

In the first place, bait fishing, as it is generally practiced, is not angling. Most bait fishermen use inadequate tackle, little or no applied intelligence, and no technique whatever. A steel pole—usually the telescopic, self-rusting variety, that is bought in the spring and thrown away in the fall—a cheap line, any old kind of a reel, and a folder of Cincinnati bass hooks; that is the typical outfit. How, I ask you, can a man turn out an angling job with such tackle? Yet that combination is practically standard equipment on the bass rivers of Pennsylvania and New York.

The two best bass rivers that I know are the Delaware and the North Branch of the Susquehanna. Both of these streams flow through well-populated country. As might be expected, both of them are heavily fished. Yet these streams continue to

Black Bass

hold better than ample supplies of bass, year after year, despite the increasingly heavy rod pressure.

Between the cities of Towanda and Wilkes-Barre, Pennsylvania, there are about forty miles of good bass water in the North Branch. This is big water and it holds big grown-up bass. In that forty-mile stretch there are literally thousands of Smallmouth that will weigh from three pounds up—how far up I don't know, but bass have been taken from that part of the river that have topped the seven-pound mark. Every one of the lovely pools in that forty miles holds its full quota of big bass. I have seen them rising to the Mayfly hatches and chasing minnows in the shallows, and believe me, they are there in considerable quantity.

There is no lack of boats in the North Branch. Every pool is well supplied with them and they are almost in constant use by bait fishermen. Yet a four pounder that is brought in to any one of the boat docks is received with high acclaim. The news spreads and summer campers flock around to inspect the unusual catch. This, mind you, in a river where there are more four pounders than in any other river I know.

One of the grudges that I hold against bait fishermen is the damage that they do annually to our supply of small bass. Hardly a day passes when I am on one of our rivers that I do not see at least one, and usually more, small bass drifting along, their gills torn loose by the careless removal of bait hooks. That is inexcusable, but it happens every day. Not only that, but the average bait dunker is delighted if he can bring in his limit of ten- and eleven-inch fish. Little bass, if they are allowed to, will grow up and furnish some of the finest sport to be found on our inland waters. But the great majority of bait fishermen don't fish for sport—they want meat. Sure, I know, I'm apt to be somewhat vitriolic when I get to talking about bait fishing, but I see so much damage done and so little sportsmanship displayed by these fellows that I can't help getting hot under the collar now and then.

Bait Fishing for Bass

When Dick was a little fellow, ten years old, I began to take him with me to the upper Delaware. He was too small to handle a bass bug and too young to leave alone on a bass river, so for several years he and I fished bait. Minnows and stone catfish are too much trouble to keep alive and carry. Crawdads are too hard to get. We couldn't quite bring ourselves to use little frogs. So we carried bait cans in our creels and fished with helgramites. They are about as productive as any of the live baits, anyway.

While I find it unpleasant to say so, there is one thing about bait fishing that is very much in its favor. For the instruction of a small boy in the vagaries of a bass river, I don't think there is any better method than to equip him with a fly rod and a can of helgramites and then let him do his own prospecting. I outfitted Dick with decent tackle, gave him preliminary instructions, and then let him learn the hard way, by trial and error. Throughout the first season, he failed to catch one legal bass. Of course, he took heavy toll among the chub and panfish, but he caught only small bass. These I taught him to unhook carefully, showing him how to cut off the hook rather than to risk injuring a small fish. I, fishing near him, managed to catch enough bass for both of us, and gradually Dick learned where bass live and where they don't live in a river. After his first disastrous attempts at casting a long line, he learned how to get his helgramite out to midriver without tearing its collar or snapping it off the hook. When he was twelve years old, he could handle a helgramite with the best of them and take more than his share of bass.

One day we parked the car near the schoolhouse pool in the Delaware below Deposit, and walked down the bank only to find four bait fishermen lined up in formation at the foot of the riffle, two on each side of the river. Like most bait fishermen, they had cheap outfits. They stood in one spot, using about rod length of line and letting their baits settle to the bottom and remain where they landed. I asked them if they would mind if we started fishing below them and worked our way downriver. They told us to go ahead—plenty of room for everybody.

I crossed the riffle above them while Dick waited on the bank until I waded in opposite him. Then we began to fish our way down through the pool. I had taught him how to fish helgramites—cast across and slightly up; then allow the bait to drift, keeping it always in motion. As soon as it began to drag on bottom, pick up and recast. Dick hooked a bass on his second cast and, while he was landing it, I hooked one. They were average Delaware bass, eleven or twelve inches long. We didn't want any fish that day so we released them, to the evident surprise of the quartet under the riffle. Before we had gone fifty feet, we had hooked and released seven fish. At last one of the quartet could stand the pressure no longer.

"Hey, kid," he called, "what kind o'bait you usin'?"

"Helgramites," replied Dick.

"Well fer Christ's sake! That's what *we're* usin' an' we ain't caught a goddam fish."

Dick didn't comment on that, nor did I. Instead we fished our way down through the pool, taking a bass now and then, and leaving the quartet to ponder on the ways of bass with a helgramite, and crazy fishermen who caught fish only to release them again.

So long as I feel as I do about bait fishing and bait fishermen, no doubt you are wondering why I'm writing this chapter. Frankly, I'm doing it under protest. For a while I had determined *not* to write such a chapter. Then, on more sober and continued reflection, I concluded that there is little that I can say here that would have the slightest influence in turning a confirmed bait fisherman toward the use of more sportsmanlike and productive methods. On the other hand, if I were to show how bait fishing can be done more effectively, this

Bait Fishing for Bass

may serve to improve the general status and to eliminate, to a small extent, some of the abuses.

Of course I have no way of knowing how you, who happen to be reading this, feel about bait fishing. The best I can do is to call my shots as I see them and hope for the best. All right, this is the way I see them.

In the first place, to do bait fishing effectively you should have good tackle. Throw away that steel pole and get yourself a fly rod, at least nine feet long and not too stiff. You can cast a bait better with a limber rod and you will hook a lot more fish.

Next, get yourself a good single-action reel. If you persist in using an automatic, sooner or later you will latch onto that bass of your dreams and he'll smash your outfit to hellangone purely because your reel won't pay out enough line to let him run.

Don't bother with a cheap line. You can't cast a cheap line any distance to speak of and it is just as important to get a bait away from you as it is to fish an artificial lure at a respectful distance. Of course, you want a sinking line. Get a braided-silk line, enameled or "vacuum dressed"—a fly-casting line, preferably tapered. A level line will do, but a tapered line will add distance to your cast and turn a light bait over nicely for you. Then, if you want to handle your big fish safely, as you probably do, fill your reel to capacity with twelve-pound nylon backing. If you can wind on one hundred yards of backing, so much the better. Then, when and if you get a big bass on, you will have line enough to let him go when and where he wishes.

Most folks use leaders that are much too heavy. Not only do heavy leaders impede the action of your bait; also there is always the risk of losing your entire casting line and backing if your leader happens to have a higher break test than the rest of your tackle. Always, just as a factor of safety, I use a leader that has a break test that is two pounds lighter than my backing. Then, in the event that I come off second best with a heavy fish, I'm sure to hang onto my line and backing.

Don't buy snelled hooks. Of all the unnatural-looking contraptions with which to adorn a choice item of bass food, a snelled hook is about the worst imaginable. And don't think for a minute that bass aren't hook- and leader-shy. Big bass certainly and most definitely are.

A good many years ago, when Dick was a little fellow and we lived in Rye, New York, we drove up into Connecticut to fish for bass in Derby Pond. This is a small lake, privately owned, and well supplied with Smallmouth.

Since Dick was only nine or ten at the time, we fished with bait—golden shiners that we seined from the shallows. The fishing was dull, so at last we decided to call it a day. Before lifting the anchor, I opened the well under the rower's seat and tossed the remaining bait fish into the lake. Some few of these were alive but perhaps fifteen or twenty of them either had given up the ghost or were in the final stages of collapse. These, of course, floated at the surface.

As we rowed away from there, we were astonished to see a school of big bass feeding actively on the dead shiners that we had left behind. In less time than it takes to tell it, these fish cleaned up every single dead shiner that we had tossed overboard.

Somewhat stimulated, we rowed back to the shallows and seined some more minnows. These we allowed to die on the bottom of the boat as we rowed back to our former location. The unfortunate shiners were then dumped over the side and the boat drifted away. While we were still within easy casting range, the bass once more came in and went to work on the shiners that were drifting on the surface. When they were well occupied with their feast, I cast my hook, baited with an almost defunct shiner, into their midst. They continued with their feeding until the last unattached shiner was consumed,

Bait Fishing for Bass

but not one single bass paid the slightest attention to the shiner on my hook.

Then we began to experiment. Using dead shiners for decoys, we tried live shiners, half-alive shiners, and dead shiners. We tried hiding the hook completely well down inside the shiner's body. We tried reducing leader size down to hair-fine 4x. We tried fishing deep and fishing shallow. We tried trolling in a circle, now and then dropping dead shiners over the side as chum. At the end of an hour of experimentation, the bass had consumed every single one of the unencumbered shiners and neither of us had had even an intimation of a nibble. So long as there was a leader attached to a shiner they would have nothing to do with it. At last, in desperation, I tore the dead shiner from my hook and threw it, as hard as I could, at the school. Smash! A big bass had it and was gone. Then we went home. As I say, live bait is not the way to catch big bass.

Of course, if you are going to catch bass there must be some sort of connecting link between your bait and your casting line. While nylon is handy stuff and works wonderfully well with bass bugs, I prefer black leaders for bait fishing. I don't know why, but black leaders seem to get better results—black gut leaders. A friend of mine uses nylon, but to the end of it he ties about two feet of black silk casting line. He claims that the soft line across the nose of a fish alarms it far less than a stiff leader. He probably is right about that. I do know that he catches his share of fish.

Another thing—have your leader long enough to keep your fly-casting line out of sight. Having a wary fish see the leader is bad enough. That can't be helped. But a casting line which, to him, must look like a tow rope, makes matters far worse.

Most people use hooks that are much too large. At best, a hook impaled in a bait is a tip-off that all is not as it should be. The more obtrusive the hook, the louder the warning. Buy number-six or number-four hooks of good quality—hollow

Black Bass

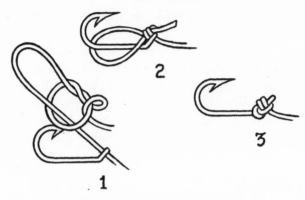

The Turle knot is good for bait hooks. Either with gut or nylon, it never slips if it is pulled tight when tied.

point, turned-down eye, and with a *very short shank*. Tie this short-shanked hook to your leader with a Turle knot. Test it after you tie the knot to ensure against leader failure. Then, when you bait up, your hook is practically hidden in the bait and your offering presents a more natural appearance. Don't worry about small fish swallowing a small hook. Little bass will swallow a number-one Cincinnati bass hook just as easily as they will a small one. If you happen to hook a little bass deeply, cut off the leader next to the eye and let him go. The chemical action of his natural body juices will decompose the hook in a matter of days and he will soon be as good as ever. If you try to unhook him, you have saved a two-cent hook and killed a bass that is worth a dollar at any hatchery. It is very little trouble to tie on a fresh hook. That's one of the nice things about buying loose hooks. They take up very little room in your kit and you can save a lot of fish if you use them as suggested.

The most popular bass baits are insect larvae, which include helgramites, dragon-fly larvae, and damsel-fly larvae, these last two combining under the group name "bass bugs"; minnows; stone catfish; crawfish or "crawdads"; frogs; newts or "lizards"; and angleworms. To be sure, folks use grass-hoppers, borers or grubs, crickets, mice, and all sorts of things, but the more common baits are those first named. Let's take a look at the way to carry and handle these most popular baits. Helgramites and "bass bugs" are best kept in wet grass, leaves, or moss. They require little care and stay lively almost indefinitely if they are kept in a ventilated container and, just as important, out of the sun and away from heat. For that reason we carry our bait cans in our creels where they are shaded and dipped in water now and then when we wade deeply.

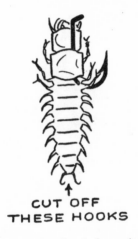

**CUT OFF
THESE HOOKS**

How to hook a helgramite

Most bait fishermen hook a helgramite incorrectly. They slide a hook carelessly under the collar and let it go at that. This, as often as not, punctures the membrane sac and the bait soon dies. The way to hook a helgramite so that he will live and cast well is to slide the point of the hook down from the top of the *side* of the collar, bringing it out through the tough skin of the top body tentacle. This prevents the hook from tearing its way through the collar and a helgramite so hooked not only stays lively but casts almost as easily as a fly. The moment a helgramite touches bottom his first instinct is to crawl under a rock. To do this he uses the tiny hooks at the end of his abdomen. If you cut these hooks off, being careful not to puncture the abdominal cavity, he will give you a lot less trouble snagging your rig on the bottom. Bass bugs should be hooked through the abdomen, lengthwise. That way small fish have trouble stealing them. This is true also of grasshoppers. Don't hook any insects or insect larvae through the thorax. Not only will they die quickly but they tear off all too easily if you hook them that way.

How to hook a minnow

Minnows, having tender mouths, are best hooked through the top of the back muscle. Pass the hook through under the dorsal fin, being careful not to injure the spine. We used to carry minnows in a standard bait pail, with the bouyant screen "bucket" that can be hung over the side of the boat. When keeping minnows or catfish overnight, don't place the wire screen bucket in a cold spring. These are warm-water fish and they will sometimes die if the spring is too chilly.

Stone catfish are hardier than minnows and much easier to keep. During most of the fishing season, the bass seem to prefer them to minnows, so they are used almost exclusively on the rivers of Pennsylvania and New York. Only in the late

Bait Fishing for Bass

How to hook a stone catfish

fall do the bass take minnows more readily. The lips of a "catty" are tough, so the best way to hook him is to pass the hook point through both lips. This does not injure him. He can breathe and he stays lively for a long time.

Crawfish can be kept very well in or out of water. We found that they stayed lively if we carried them in bait cans, just as we carried helgramites. When you hook a crawdad, don't hook him through the shell. If you do you will kill him right away. Pass the point of the hook through the upper part of the tail muscle, from the underside, fairly close to the shell, and bring out the point so that it lies along the top of the tail. This conceals a short-shank hook, and a crawfish so hooked will stay lively a long time. If you can get them, the "shedder" crawdads, those which are putting on a new shell, are the finest sort of bass bait. "Soft craws" some call them, and the bass really go for them in a big way. Hook them through the tail, just as you would a hardshell crawdad.

How to hook a crawdad

Black Bass

Frogs are best handled with a frog harness. We take little pleasure inflicting pain on small creatures. Thus, we did not use frogs and newts when Dick was a youngster. There were plenty of other baits that served just as well. Fish, crawdads, insects, and worms have no sense of pain. Frogs and newts have, so we let them alone.

I find, in looking over the foregoing, that I neglected to mention lamphrey eels. These young eels—lampers—are just as fine bass bait as you can get. Strictly speaking, lamphreys are not eels at all, but they look like eels and are referred to as such by the bait fishermen. The trouble is that they are becoming more and more scarce each year. Best hook them through the top of the tail muscle, avoiding the body cavity and the spine. They are tough little rascals, and the bass like them. These can be carried in wet moss or wet grass but, after all, they are fish and are best carried in a bait pail.

How to hook an angleworm. If you want him to stay lively, don't hook him through the collar.

Angleworms, of course, can be carried in earth, wet grass, moss, or what have you. Keep them away from heat and they will last for days. When you hook an angleworm, don't hook him through the collar. That is the center of his vital organs and he will die rather quickly. Best hook him through the abdomen, just below the collar, hiding as much as you can of the hook. Don't loop him on the hook—let head and tail hang free. That way he will stay lively for a long time.

Remember, when you are bait fishing, that you are, in

Bait Fishing for Bass

effect, a salesman. Apply approved sales methods. There is a great deal of difference between selling and merely having something for sale. Most bait fishermen fall into the latter class. They are content merely to plop their baits out into the water and then wait for the customers to come to them. They don't even bother to provide a good show window to display goods. Instead, they allow their baits to settle where they may, and then patiently to stand, or sit, and hope for the best. That, obviously, is not the way to sell anything, be it brushes or five-foot shelves or life insurance or fish bait.

Unless you are in a known, proven concentration spot where there are plenty of bass and you have fast action, it is never wise to anchor your boat or to stand in one spot. Keep moving, slowly and quietly but always moving, so that you can be sure to show your wares to the maximum number of customers. That way you will get action while the stationary fisherman does not. In a river, either wade slowly downstream or let the current carry your boat. In a lake, let the wind take you along. Either way you can move quietly, and that is important.

When you are fishing a river, remember that the majority of the "open-water" bass are to be found in the main current, under the "thread of the stream" or "feeding lane." The bubbles and foam from the riffles will usually mark this area quite plainly for you. Thus, it is wise to confine your operations to this feeding lane.

In a river, if we were wading, we cast up and across, keeping the bait always in evidence and in motion. If we were in a boat, we cast to the side, cross-current, and slightly ahead of our drift, so that bait and boat moved along with the current at the same rate. Don't use sinkers or floats; you don't need them in a river. A sinker takes your bait to the bottom too fast and a float encumbers your casting and prevents natural action on the part of your bait. Simply cast out to the side and let the bait do what it will until it touches bottom. Then

Black Bass

pick up and recast. Stone catfish and minnows often will swim about and stay free of the bottom for a long time. Crawfish, helgramites, bass bugs, and such will, of course, sink rather quickly and must be recast frequently.

It is not uncommon to see fishermen drifting along in a boat, their baits dragging along on bottom behind them, directly in the area that has just been passed over by the boat. It is not surprising that these fellows get very few big bass. I have always been of the opinion that if a big bass sees you or knows that you are in his general vicinity, your chances of getting him are reduced practically to zero. That is the reason for casting to the side, as far as possible from the boat, as you thus show your bait to undisturbed fish.

When a bait fisherman gets a "strike," the bass picks up the bait and starts off with it. The accepted procedure is to pay out line until the "run-out" stops. Then the fish is occupied with turning the bait so that it can be swallowed head first. So far, so good. Don't be guilty of waiting quietly until the fish starts off again. When that happens, particularly in the case of small fish, more often than not the hook has been swallowed. Instead of waiting for a bass to move after he has stopped to turn the bait, strip in line quietly until you can feel the fish. Then strike—not with a sudden jerk but with a firm pulling-in of the barb. That way you will hook just as many and do far less damage among the small fry.

Of course, with the smaller baits—helgramites, bass bugs, small crawdads, small minnows, and such—you don't need to bother with paying out line for the "run-out." When the fish starts away with your bait, simply wait until he comes up against tight line; then pull the barb home. Usually you will find him hooked in the tough membrane at the corner of his mouth.

Some years ago, Bill Randebrock introduced me to a method of fishing a shallow Largemouth lake. The night before I arrived, he had labored diligently collecting a copious

Bait Fishing for Bass

supply of monster "nightwalkers" or "dew worms"—the oversize angleworms that crawl about on any well-watered lawn after dark. The next day, equipped with fly rods, a landing net, a supply of bait hooks, the box of nightwalkers, and some cork floats, we drove to a Largemouth lake near his home. We hired a boat and Bill rowed to the upwind end of the lake. There he showed me how to rig my tackle. The lines, leaders, and hooks were all conventional bait-fishing gear. About three feet above the hook, a cork float was attached to the leader, this to keep our nightwalkers clear of encumberance with lake bottom or weeds. Each of us baited up with a huge nightwalker and shoved off. The game was to strip-cast the nightwalkers well ahead of the boat and then slowly strip in line as the wind blew the boat up to our cork floats. When we came too close to the floats, we would pick up and recast. It took a bit of gentle handling to cast a nightwalker thirty-five or forty feet ahead of the boat, but I soon found that it could be done.

There were plenty of panfish in the lake and these feasted royally on big nightwalkers, but now and then a Largemouth would take one of our baits. During the course of the afternoon we picked up eight or ten very nice bass. I don't imagine that most of these fish had so much as seen a nightwalker prior to that day but that made no difference. They really took them actively, this in a hard-fished lake on the outskirts of the New York metropolitan area. As a matter of fact, we could see the Empire State Building from the bank of the lake.

Up in Georgian Bay, Ontario, the almost universal bait is the minnow. Probably the reason for this is the fact that minnows are so easy to catch. Under the dock at Camp Mordolphton, Birch Island, Ontario, there are thousands of minnows, ready and willing to be dipped up when wanted. A can of oatmeal and a dip net are kept handy on the dock. When you want a mess of bass bait, simply lower the dip net over the side, sprinkle some oatmeal into the water, wait a minute or so, and then raise the net. One dip and you are provided with bait for the day.

The choice spots for bait fishing in that territory are, of course, the backwaters immediately adjoining the thorough-fares between the islands. Here the bass congregate. The guide anchors the boat in the backwater and operations begin. The first move is to place a ringed sinker over the point of your hook and lower it over the side until it touches bottom. Then mark the depth of the water on your line by tying onto it a small piece of wrapping twine. This will slide through the guides, whereas a cork float that is placed at that spot makes hand lining necessary in landing fish. No sinker is used. The minnows are hooked under their dorsal fins and allowed to swim about as they choose, their maximum depth being con-trolled by the twine marker on your line. This sort of fishing isn't really very much fun, but it is entirely possible to fill a boat with bass if you care to ignore the game laws and do so. We put in one day at this sort of nonsense—then we went after Largemouth in the coves and enjoyed ourselves thoroughly.

As I said at the start of this chapter, I have no use for bait fishing. Definitely, it is not the way to catch bass. A good man with a bass bug or a casting rod can turn up more big bass in a single afternoon than a bait fisherman can show you in a week or so of serious, intensive fishing. I have no reason to believe that anything I can say here will change the ideas of a confirmed bait fisherman as much as one half of one per cent. However, as I said before, I feel that I should call my shots as I see them. My advice to bait fishermen—and unso-licited advice is worth just about what the unwilling recipient pays for it—is to put away such childlike pastimes as bait fish-ing and take up seriously the job of learning to be an angler.

Good fishing!